ISBN 0-8373-0120-3

C-120   CAREER EXAMINATION SERIES

This is your
PASSBOOK® for...

Captain, Fire Department

Test Preparation Study Guide

Questions & Answers

NATIONAL LEARNING CORPORATION

Copyright © 2006 by

National Learning Corporation

212 Michael Drive, Syosset, New York 11791

(516) 921-8888
(800) 645-6337
FAX: (516) 921-8743
www.passbooks.com
email: sales @ passbooks.com
info @ passbooks.com

PRINTED IN THE UNITED STATES OF AMERICA

PASSBOOK®

NOTICE

PASSBOOK SERIES®

THE *PASSBOOK SERIES*® has been created to prepare applicants and candidates for the ultimate academic battlefield—the examination room.

At some time in our lives, each and every one of us may be required to take an examination—for validation, matriculation, admission, qualification, registration, certification, or licensure.

Based on the assumption that every applicant or candidate has met the basic formal educational standards, has taken the required number of courses, and read the necessary texts, the *PASSBOOK SERIES*® furnishes the one special preparation which may assure passing with confidence, instead of failing with insecurity. Examination questions—together with answers—are furnished as the basic vehicle for study so that the mysteries of the examination and its compounding difficulties may be eliminated or diminished by a sure method.

This book is meant to help you pass your examination provided that you qualify and are serious in your objective.

The entire field is reviewed through the huge store of content information which is succinctly presented through a provocative and challenging approach—the question-and-answer method.

A climate of success is established by furnishing the correct answers at the end of each test.

You soon learn to recognize types of questions, forms of questions, and patterns of questioning. You may even begin to anticipate expected outcomes.

You perceive that many questions are repeated or adapted so that you gain acute insights, which may enable you to score many sure points.

You learn how to confront new questions, or types of questions, and to attack them confidently and work out the correct answers.

You note objectives and emphases, and recognize pitfalls and dangers, so that you may make positive educational adjustments.

Moreover, you are kept fully informed in relation to new concepts, methods, practices, and directions in the field.

You discover that you are actually taking the examination all the time: you are preparing for the examination by "taking" an examination, not by reading extraneous and/or supererogatory textbooks.

In short, this PASSBOOK®, used directedly, should be an important factor in helping you to pass your test.

CAPTAIN, FIRE DEPARTMENT

DUTIES AND RESPONSIBILITIES

Under general direction, is in responsible command of one or more fire companies or auxiliary operating units occupying a fire quarters; is responsible for the efficiency and effectiveness of his assigned company, for the administration of companies and units in fire quarters, and for the efficient management of programs to achieve department goals; performs related work.

EXAMPLES OF TYPICAL TASKS

Assumes responsibility for the efficient administration of fire quarters and commands the companies or units housed therein. Maintains the discipline of members in his command and assures the maintenance and protection of all department property in or assigned to the fire quarters. Performs all other duties prescribed for this position in the regulations of the department.

TESTS

The written test will be of the multiple-choice type and may include questions of firemanics, technical aspects of prevention and extinguishment, use and limitation of tools and equipment; principles and techniques of supervision and administration; relevant laws and codes; departmental regulations and procedures; and related subjects.

HOW TO TAKE A TEST

I. YOU MUST PASS AN EXAMINATION

A. WHAT EVERY CANDIDATE SHOULD KNOW

Examination applicants often ask us for help in preparing for the written test. What can I study in advance? What kinds of questions will be asked? How will the test be given? How will the papers be graded?

As an applicant for a civil service examination, you may be wondering about some of these things. Our purpose here is to suggest effective methods of advance study and to describe civil service examinations.

Your chances for success on this examination can be increased if you know how to prepare. Those "pre-examination jitters" can be reduced if you know what to expect. You can even experience an adventure in good citizenship if you know why civil service examinations are given.

B. WHY ARE CIVIL SERVICE EXAMINATIONS GIVEN?

Civil service examinations are important to you in two ways. As a citizen, you want public jobs filled by employees who know how to do their work. As a job-seeker, you want a fair chance to compete for that job on an equal footing with other candidates. The best known means of accomplishing this two-fold goal is the competitive examination.

Examinations are widely publicized throughout the nation. They may be administered for jobs in federal, state, city, municipal, town, or village governments or agencies.

Any citizen may apply, with some limitations, such as the age or residence of applicants. Your experience and education may be reviewed to see whether you meet the requirements for the particular examination. When these requirements exist, they are reasonable and are applied consistently to all applicants. Thus, a competitive examination may cause you some uneasiness now, but it is your privilege and safeguard.

C. HOW ARE CIVIL SERVICE EXAMINATIONS DEVELOPED?

Examinations are carefully written by trained technicians who are specialists in the field known as "psychological measurement," in consultation with recognized authorities in the field of work that the test will cover. These experts recommend the subject matter areas or skills to be tested; only those knowledges or skills important to your success on the job are included. The most reliable books and source materials available are used as references. Together, the experts and technicians judge the difficulty level of the questions.

Test technicians know how to phrase questions so that the problem is clearly stated. Their ethics do not permit "trick" or "catch" questions. Questions may have been tried out on sample groups, or subjected to statistical analysis, to determine their usefulness.

Written tests are often used in combination with performance tests, ratings of training and experience, and oral interviews. All of these measures combine to form the best known means of finding the right man for the right job.

II. HOW TO PASS THE WRITTEN TEST
A. *NATURE OF THE EXAMINATION*

To prepare intelligently for civil service examinations, you should know how they differ from school examinations you have taken. In school you were assigned certain definite pages to read or subjects to cover. The examination questions were quite detailed and usually emphasized memory. Civil service examinations, on the other hand, try to discover your present ability to perform the duties of a position, plus your potentiality to learn these duties. In other words, a civil service examination attempts to predict how successful you will be. Questions cover such a broad area that they cannot be as minute and detailed as school examination questions.

In the public service similar kinds of work, or positions, are grouped together in one "class." This process is known as "position-classification." All the positions in a class are paid according to the salary range for that class. One class title covers all these positions, and they are all tested by the same examination.

B. *FOUR BASIC STEPS*

1. Study the Announcement.--How, then, can you know what subjects to study? Our best answer is: "Learn as much as possible about the class of positions for which you have applied." The examination will test the knowledge, skills, and abilities needed to do the work.

Your most valuable source of information about the position you want is the official announcement of the examination. This announcement lists the training and experience qualifications. Check these standards and apply only if you come reasonably close to meeting them.

The brief description of the position in the examination announcement offers some clues to the subjects which will be tested. Think about the job itself. Review the duties in your mind. Can you perform them, or are there some in which you are rusty? Fill in the blank spots in your preparation.

Many jurisdictions preview the written test in the examination announcement by including a section called "Knowledge and Abilities Required," "Scope of Examination," or some similar heading. Here you will find out specifically what fields will be tested.

2. Review Your Own Background.-- Once you learn in general what the position is all about, and what you need to know to do the work, ask yourself which subjects you already know fairly well and which need improvement. You may wonder whether to concentrate on improving your strong areas or on building some background in your fields of weakness. When the announcement has specified "some knowledge" or "considerable knowledge," or has used adjectives such as "beginning principles of ...." or "advanced .....methods," you can get a clue as to the number and difficulty of questions to be asked in any given field. More questions, and hence broader coverage, would be included for those subjects which are more important in the work. Now weigh your strengths and weaknesses against the job requirements and prepare accordingly.

3. Determine the Level of the Position.-- Another way to tell how intensively you should prepare is to understand the level of the job for which you are applying. Is it the entering level? In other words, is this the position in which beginners in a field of work are hired? Or is it an intermediate or advanced level? Sometimes this is indicated by such words as "Junior" or "Senior" in the class title.Other jurisdictions use Roman numerals to designate the level: Clerk I,

Clerk II, for example. The word "Supervisor" sometimes appears in the title. If the level is not indicated by the title, check the description of duties. Will you be working under very close supervision, or will you have responsibility for independent decisions in this work?

4. Choose Appropriate Study Materials.-- Now that you know the subjects to be examined and the relative amount of each subject to be covered, you can choose suitable study materials. For beginning level jobs, or even advanced ones, if you have a pronounced weakness in some aspect of your training, read a modern, standard textbook in that field. Be sure it is up-to-date and has general coverage. Such books are normally available at your library, and the librarian will be glad to help you locate one. For entry level positions, questions of appropriate difficulty are chosen -- neither highly advanced questions, nor those too simple. Such questions require careful thought but not advanced training.

If the position for which you are applying is technical or advanced, you will read more advanced, specialized material. If you are already familiar with the basic principles of your field, elementary textbooks would waste your time. Concentrate on advanced textbooks and technical periodicals. Think through the concepts and review difficult problems in your field.

These are all general sources. You can get more ideas on your own initiative, following these leads. For example, training manuals and publications of the government agency which employs workers in your field can be useful, particularly for technical and professional positions. A letter or visit to the government department involved may result in more specific study suggestions, and certainly will provide you with a more definite idea of the exact nature of the position you are seeking.

III. KINDS OF TESTS

Tests are used for purposes other than measuring knowledge and ability to perform specified duties. For some positions, it is equally important to test ability to make adjustments to new situations or to profit from training. In others, basic mental abilities not dependent upon information are essential. Questions which test these things may not appear as pertinent to the duties of the position as those which test for knowledge and information. Yet they are often highly important parts of a fair examination. For very general questions, it is almost impossible to help you direct your study efforts. What we can do is to point out some of the more common of these general abilities needed in public service positions and describe some typical questions.

1. General Information

Broad, general information has been found useful for predicting job success in some kinds of work. This is tested in a variety of ways, from vocabulary lists to questions about current events. Basic background in some field of work, such as sociology or economics, may be sampled in a group of questions. Often these are principles which have become familiar to most persons through "exposure" rather than through formal training. It is difficult to advise you how to study for these questions; being alert to the world around you is our best suggestion.

3

2. Verbal Ability

An example of an ability needed in many positions is verbal or language ability. Verbal ability is, in brief, the ability to use and understand words. Vocabulary and grammar tests are typical measures of this ability. "Reading comprehension" or "paragraph interpretation" questions are common in many kinds of civil service tests. You are given a paragraph of written material and asked to find its central meaning.

3. Numerical Ability

Number skills can be tested by the familiar arithmetic problem, by checking paired lists of numbers to see which are alike and which are different, or by interpreting charts and graphs. In the latter test, a graph may be printed in the test booklet which you are asked to use as the basis for answering questions.

4. Observation

A popular test for law-enforcement positions is the observation test. A picture is shown to you for several minutes, then taken away. Questions about the picture test your ability to observe both details and larger elements.

5. Following Directions

In many positions in the public service, the employee must be able to carry out written instructions dependably and accurately. You may be given a chart with several columns, each column listing a variety of information. The questions require you to carry out directions involving the information given in the chart.

6. Skills and Aptitudes

Performance tests effectively measure some manual skills and aptitudes. When the skill is one in which you are trained, such as typing or shorthand, you can practice. These tests are often very much like those given in business school or high school courses. For many of the other skills and aptitudes, however, no short-time preparation can be made. Skills and abilities natural to you or that you have developed throughout your lifetime are being tested.

Many of the general questions just described provide all the data needed to answer the questions and ask you to use your reasoning ability to find the answers. Your best preparation for these tests, as well as for tests of facts and ideas, is to be at your physical and mental best. You, no doubt, have your own methods of getting into an exam-taking mood and keeping "in shape." The next section lists some ideas on this subject.

IV. KINDS OF QUESTIONS

Only rarely is the "essay" question, which you answer in narrative form, used in civil service tests. Civil service tests are usually of the short-answer type. Full instructions for answering these questions will be given to you at the examination. But in case this is your first experience with short-answer questions and separate answer sheets, here is what you need to know.

1. Multiple-Choice Questions

Most popular of the short-answer questions is the "multiple-choice" or "best-answer" question. It can be used, for example, to test for factual knowledge, ability to solve problems, or judgment in meeting situations found at work.

A multiple-choice question is normally one of three types:

(1) It can begin with an incomplete statement followed by several possible endings. You are to find the one ending which *best* completes the statement, although some of the others may not be entirely wrong.

(2) It can also be a complete statement in the form of a question which is answered by choosing one of the statements listed.

(3) It can be in the form of a problem -- again you select the best answer.

Here is an example of a multiple-choice question with a discussion which should give you some clues as to the method for choosing the right answer.

SAMPLE QUESTION:

When an employee has a complaint about his assignment, the action which will *best* help him overcome his difficulty is

    (A) to discuss his difficulty with his co-workers

    (B) to take the problem to the head of the organization

    (C) to take the problem to the person who gave him the assignment

    (D) to say nothing to anyone about his complaint

In answering this question you should study each of the choices to find which is best. Consider choice (A). Certainly an employee may discuss his complaint with fellow employees, but no change or improvement can result, and the complaint remains unsolved. Choice (B) is a poor choice since the head of the organization probably does not know what assignment you have been given, and taking your problem to him is known as "going over the head" of the supervisor. The supervisor, or person who made the assignment, is the person who can clarify it or correct any injustice. Choice (C) is, therefore, correct. To say nothing, as in choice (D), is unwise. Supervisors have an interest in knowing the problems employees are facing, and the employee is seeking a solution to his problem.

  2. True-False Questions

The "true-false" or "right-wrong" form of question is sometimes used. Here a complete statement is given. Your problem is to decide whether the statement is right or wrong.

SAMPLE QUESTION:

A person-to-person long distance telephone call costs less than a station-to-station call to the same city.

This question is wrong, or "false," since person-to-person calls are more expensive.

This is not a complete list of all possible question forms, although most of the others are variations of these common types. You will always get complete directions for answering questions. Be sure you understand *how* to mark your answers -- ask questions until you do.

V. RECORDING YOUR ANSWERS

For an examination with very few applicants, you may be told to record your answers in the test booklet itself. Separate answer sheets are much more common. If this separate answer sheet is to be scored by machine -- and this is often the case -- it is highly important that you mark your answers correctly in order to get credit.

An electric test-scoring machine is often used in civil service offices because of the speed with which papers can be scored. Machine-scored answer sheets must be marked with a special pencil, which will be given to you. This pencil has a high graphite content which responds to the electrical scoring machine. As a matter of fact, stray dots may register as answers, so do not let your pencil rest on the answer sheet while you are pondering the correct answer. Also, if your pencil lead breaks or is otherwise defective, ask for another.

Since the answer sheet will be dropped in a slot in the scoring machine, be careful not to bend the corners or get the paper crumpled.

The answer sheet normally has five vertical columns of numbers, with 30 numbers to a column. These numbers correspond to the question numbers in your test booklet. After each number, going across the page, are four or five pairs of dotted lines. These short dotted lines have small letters or numbers above them. The first two pairs may also have a "T" and "F" above the letters. This indicates that the first two pairs only are to be used if the questions are of the true-false type. If the questions are multiple-choice, disregard this "T" and "F" completely, and pay attention only to the small number or letters.

Answer your questions in the manner of the sample that follows. Proceed in the sequential steps outlined below.

Assume that you are answering question 32, which is:

    32. The largest city in the United States is:
        A. Washington, D.C.   B. New York City   C. Chicago
        D. Detroit   E. San Francisco

1. Choose the answer you think is best.
    New York City is the largest, so choice B is correct.
2. Find the row of dotted lines numbered the same as the question you are answering.
    This is question number 32, so find row number 32.
3. Find the pair of dotted lines corresponding to the answer you have chosen.
    You have chosen answer B, so find the pair of dotted lines marked "B".
4. Make a solid black mark between the dotted lines.
    Go up and down two or three times with your pencil so plenty of graphite rubs off, but do not let the mark get outside or above the dots.

	T A	F B	C	D	E
29	::	::	::	::	::
30	::	::	::	::	::
31	::	::	::	::	::
32	::	▉	::	::	::
33	::	::	::	::	::

VI. BEFORE THE TEST

Common sense will help you find procedures to follow to get ready for an examination. Too many of us, however, overlook these sensible measures. Indeed, nervousness and fatigue have been found to be the most serious reasons why applicants fail to do their best on civil service tests. Here is a list of reminders.

1. Begin Your Preparation Early

Don't wait until the last minute to go scurrying around for books and materials or to find out what the position is all about.

2. Prepare Continuously

An hour a night for a week is better than an all-night cram session. This has been definitely established. What is more, a night a week for a month will return better dividends than crowding your study into a shorter period of time.

3. Locate the Place of the Examination

You have been sent a notice telling you when and where to report for the examination. If the location is in a different town or otherwise unfamiliar to you, it would be well to inquire the best route and learn something about the building.

4. Relax the Night Before the Test

Allow your mind to rest. Do not study at all that night. Plan some mild recreation or diversion; then go to bed early and get a good night's sleep.

5. Get Up Early Enough to Make a Leisurely Trip to the Place for the Test

Then unforeseen events, traffic snarls, unfamiliar buildings, will not upset you.

6. Dress Comfortably

A written test is not a fashion show. You will be known by number and not by name, so wear something comfortable.

7. Leave Excess Paraphernalia at Home

Shopping bags and odd bundles will get in your way. You need bring only the items mentioned in the official notice sent to you; usually everything you need is provided. Do not bring reference books to the examination. They will only confuse those last minutes and be taken away from you when in the test room.

8. Arrive Somewhat Ahead of Time

If because of transportation schedules you must get there very early, bring a newspaper or magazine to take your mind off yourself while waiting.

9. Locate the Examination Room

When you have found the proper room, you will be directed to the seat or part of the room where you will sit. Sometimes you are given a sheet of instructions to read while you are waiting. Do not fill out any forms until you are told to do so; just read them and be ready.

10. Relax and Prepare to Listen to the Instructions

11. If you have any physical problem that may keep you from doing your best, be sure to tell the test administrator. If you are sick, or in poor health, you really cannot do your best on the test. You can come back and take the test some other time.

VII. AT THE TEST

The day of the test is here and you have the test booklet in your hand. The temptation to get going is very strong. Caution! There is more to success than knowing the right answers. You must know how to identify your papers and understand variations in the type of short-answer question used in this particular examination. Follow these suggestions for maximum results from your efforts:

1. Cooperate with the Monitor

The test administrator has a duty to create a situation in which you can be as much at ease as possible. He will give instructions, tell you when to begin, check to see that you are marking your answer sheet correctly. He is not there to guard you, although he will see that your competitors do not take unfair advantage. He wants to help you do your best.

2. Listen to All Instructions

Don't jump the gun! Wait until you understand all directions. In most civil service tests you get more time than you need to answer the questions. So don't get in a hurry. Read each word of instructions until you clearly understand the meaning. Study the examples. Listen to all announcements. Follow directions. Ask questions if you do not understand what to do.

3. Identify Your Papers

Civil service examinations are usually identified by number only. You will be assigned a number; you must not put your name on your test papers. Be sure to copy your number correctly. Since more than one examination may be given, copy your exact examination title.

4. Plan Your Time

Unless you are told that a test is a "speed" or "rate-of-work" test, speed itself is not usually important. Time enough to answer all the questions will be provided. But this does not mean that you have all day. An overall time limit has been set. Divide the total time (in minutes) by the number of questions to get the approximate time you have for each question.

5. Do Not Linger Over Difficult Questions

If you come across a difficult question, mark it with a paper clip (useful to have along) and come back to it when you have been through the booklet. One caution if you do this -- be sure to skip a number on your answer sheet too. Check often to be sure that you have not lost your place and that you are marking in the row numbered the same as the question you are answering.

6. Read the Questions

Be sure you know what the question asks! Many capable people are unsuccessful because they failed to *read* the questions correctly.

7. Answer All Questions

Unless you have been instructed that a penalty will be deducted for incorrect answers, it is better to guess than to omit a question.

8. Speed Tests

It is often better *not* to guess on speed tests. It has been found that on timed tests people are tempted to spend the last few seconds before time is called in marking answers at random -- without even reading them -- in the hope of picking up a few extra points. To discourage this practice, the instructions may warn you that your score will be "corrected" for guessing. That is, a penalty will be applied. The incorrect answers will be deducted from the correct ones, or some other penalty formula will be used.

9. Review Your Answers

If you finish before time is called, go back to the questions you guessed or omitted to give further thought to them. Review other answers if you have time.

10. Return Your Test Materials

If you are ready to leave before others have finished or time is called, take *all* your materials to the monitor and leave quietly. Never take any test material with you. The monitor can discover whose papers are not complete, and taking a test booklet may be grounds for disqualification.

VIII. EXAMINATION TECHNIQUES

1. Read the *general* instructions carefully. These are usually printed on the first page of the examination booklet. As a rule, these instructions refer to the timing of the examination; the fact that you should not start work until the signal and must stop work at a signal, etc. If there are any *special* instructions, such as a choice of questions to be answered, make sure that you note this instruction carefully.

2. When you are ready to start work on the examination, that is as soon as the signal has been given, read the instructions to each question booklet, underline any key words or phrases, such as *least, best, outline, describe,* and the like. In this way you will tend to answer as requested rather than discover on reviewing your paper that you *listed without describing,* that you selected the *worst* choice rather than the *best* choice, etc.

3. If the examination is of the objective or so-called multiple-choice type, that is, each question will also give a series of possible answers: A, B, C, or D, and you are called upon to select the best answer and write the letter next to that answer on your answer paper, it is advisable to start answering each question in turn. There may be anywhere from 50 to 100 such questions in the three or four hours allotted and you can see how much time would be taken if you read through all the questions before beginning to answer any. Furthermore, if you come across a question or a group of questions which you know would be difficult to answer, it would undoubtedly affect your handling of all the other questions.

4. If the examination is of the esssay-type and contains but a few questions, it is a moot point as to whether you should read all the questions before starting to answer any one. Of course if you are given a choice, say five out of seven and the like, then it is essential to read all the questions so you can eliminate the two which are most difficult. If, however, you are asked to answer all the questions, there may be danger in trying to answer the easiest one first because you may find that you will spend too much time on it. The best technique is to answer the first question, then proceed to the second, etc.

5. Time your answers. Before the examination begins, write down the time it started, then add the time allowed for the examination and write down the time it must be completed, then divide the time available somewhat as follows:

(a) If $3\frac{1}{2}$ hours are allowed, that would be 210 minutes. If you have 80 objective-type questions, that would be an average of $2\frac{1}{2}$ minutes per question. Allow yourself no more than 2 minutes per question, or a total of 160 minutes, which will permit about 50 minutes to review.

(b) If for the time allotment of 210 minutes, there are 7 essay questions to answer, that would average about 30 minutes a question. Give yourself only 25 minutes per question so that you have about 35 minutes to review.

6. The most important instruction is *to read each question* and make sure you know what is wanted. The second most important instruction is to *time yourself properly* so that you answer every question. The third most important instruction is to *answer every question.* Guess if you have to but include something for each question. Remember that you will receive no credit for a blank and will probably receive some credit if you write something in answer to an essay question. If you guess a letter, say "B" for a multiple-choice question, you may have guessed right. If you leave a blank as the answer to a multiple-choice question, the examiners may respect your feelings but it will not add a point to your score.

7. Suggestions
  a. Objective-Type Questions
    (1) Examine the question booklet for proper sequence of pages and questions.
    (2) Read all instructions carefully.
    (3) Skip any question which seems too difficult; return to it after all other questions have been answered.
    (4) Apportion your time properly; do not spend too much time on any single question or group of questions.
    (5) Note and underline key words -- *all, most, fewest, least, best, worst, same, opposite.*
    (6) Pay particular attention to negatives.
    (7) Note unusual option, e.g., unduly long, short, complex, different or similar in content to the body of the question.
    (8) Observe the use of "hedging" words -- *probably, may, most likely, etc.*
    (9) Make sure that your answer is put next to the same number as the question.
    (10) Do not second-guess unless you have good reason to believe the second answer is definitely more correct.
    (11) Cross out original answer if you decide another answer is more accurate; do not erase.
    (12) Answer all questions; guess unless instructed otherwise.
    (13) Leave time for review.
  b. Essay-Type Questions
    (1) Read each question carefully.
    (2) Determine exactly what is wanted. Underline key words or phrases.
    (3) Decide on outline or paragraph answer.
    (4) Include many different points and elements unless asked to develop any one or two points or elements.
    (5) Show impartiality by giving pros and cons unless directed to select one side only.
    (6) Make and write down any assumptions you find necessary to answer the question.
    (7) Watch your English, grammar, punctuation, choice of words.
    (8) Time your answers; don't crowd material.

8. Answering the Essay Question
    Most essay questions can be answered by framing the specific response around several key words or ideas. Here are a few such key words or ideas:

M's: manpower,materials, methods, money, management;
P's: purpose, program, policy, plan, procedure, practice, problems, pitfalls, personnel, public relations.

a. Six Basic Steps in Handling Problems:
   (1) Preliminary plan and background development
   (2) Collect information, data and facts
   (3) Analyze and interpret information, data and facts
   (4) Analyze and develop solutions as well as make recommendations
   (5) Prepare report and sell recommendations
   (6) Install recommendations and follow up effectiveness

b. Pitfalls to Avoid
   (1) *Taking things for granted*
       A statement of the situation does not necessarily imply that each of the elements is necessarily true; for example, a complaint may be invalid and biased so that all that can be taken for granted is that a complaint has been registered.
   (2) *Considering only one side of a situation*
       Wherever possible, indicate several alternatives and then point out the reasons you selected the best one.
   (3) *Failing to indicate follow-up*
       Whenever your answer indicates action on your part, make certain that you will take proper follow-up action to see how successful your recommendations, procedures, or actions turn out to be.
   (4) *Taking too long in answering any single question*
       Remember to time your answers properly.

IX. AFTER THE TEST
   Scoring procedures differ in detail among civil service jurisdictions although the general principles are the same. Whether the papers are hand-scored or graded by the electric scoring machine we have described, they are nearly always graded by number. That is, the person who marks the paper knows only the number -- never the name -- of the applicant. Not until all the papers have been graded will they be matched with names. If other tests, such as training and experience or oral interview ratings have been given, scores will be combined. Different parts of the examination usually have different weights. For example, the written test might count 60 percent of the final grade, and a rating of training and experience 40 percent. In many jurisdictions, veterans will have a certain number of points added to their grades.

   After the final grade has been determined, the names are placed in grade order and an eligible list is established. There are various methods for resolving ties between those who get the same final grade: probably the most common is to place first the name of the person whose application was received first. Job offers are made from the eligible list in the order the names appear on it.

   You will be notified of your grade and your rank order as soon as all these computations have been made. This will be done as rapidly as possible.

   People who are found to meet the requirements in the announcement are called "eligibles." Their names are put on a list of eligibles. An eligible's chances of getting a job depend on how high he stands on this list and how fast agencies are filling jobs from the list.

When a job is to be filled from a list of eligibles, the agency asks for the names of people on the list of eligibles for that job.

When the civil service commission receives this request, it sends to the agency the names of the three people highest on the list. Or, if the job to be filled has specialized requirements, the office sends the agency, from the general list, the names of the top three persons who meet those requirements.

The appointing officer makes a choice from among the three people whose names were sent to him. If the selected person accepts the appointment, the names of the others are put back on the list to be considered for future openings.

That is the rule in hiring from all kinds of eligible lists, whether they are for typist, carpenter, chemist, or something else. For every vacancy, the appointing officer has his choice of any one of the top three eligibles on the list. This explains why the person whose name is on top of the list sometimes does not get an appointment when some of the persons lower on the list do. If the appointing officer chooses the No.2 or No.3 eligible, the No.1 eligible does not get a job at once, but stays on the list until he is appointed or the list is terminated.

X. HOW TO PASS THE INTERVIEW TEST

The examination for which you applied requires an oral interview test. You have already taken the written test and you are now being called for the interview test -- the final part of the formal examination.

You may think that it is not possible to prepare for an interview test and that there are no procedures to follow during an interview.

Our purpose is to point out some things you can do in advance that will help you and some good rules to follow and pitfalls to avoid while you are being interviewed.

A. *WHAT IS AN INTERVIEW SUPPOSED TO TEST?*

The written examination is designed to test the technical knowledge and competence of the candidate; the oral is designed to evaluate intangible qualities, not readily measured otherwise, and to establish a list showing the relative fitness of each candidate, *as measured against his competitors*, for the position sought. Scoring is not on the basis of "right" or "wrong," but on a sliding scale of values ranging from "not passable" to "outstanding." As a matter of fact, it is possible to achieve a relatively low score without a single "incorrect" answer because of evident weakness in the qualities being measured,

Occasionally, an examination may consist entirely of an oral test -- either an individual or a group oral. In such cases, information is sought concerning the technical knowledges and abilities of the candidate, since there has been no written examination for this purpose. More commonly, however, an oral test is used to supplement a written examination.

B. *WHO CONDUCTS INTERVIEWS?*

The composition of oral boards varies among different jurisdictions. In nearly all, a representative of the personnel department serves as chairman. One of the members of the board may be a representative of the department in which the candidate would work. In some cases, "outside experts" are used, and, frequently, a business man or some other representative of the general public is asked to serve. Labor and management or other special groups may be represented. The aim is to secure the services of experts in the appropriate field.

However the board is composed, it is a good idea (and not at all improper or unethical) to ascertain in advance of the interview who the members are and what groups they represent. When you are introduced to them, you will have some idea of their backgrounds and interests, and at least you will not stutter and stammer over their names.

C. WHAT TO DO BEFORE THE INTERVIEW

While knowledge about the board members is useful and takes some of the surprise element out of the interview, there is other preparation which is more substantive. It *is* possible to prepare for an oral -- in several ways:

1. Keep a Copy of Your Application and Review it Carefully Before the Interview

   This may be the only document before the oral board, and the starting point of the interview. Know what experience and education you have listed there, and the sequence and dates of it. Sometimes the board will ask *you* to review the highlights of your experience for them; you should not have to hem and haw doing it.

2. Study the Class Specification and the Examination Announcement

   Usually, the oral board has one or both of these to guide them. The qualities, characteristics, or knowledges required by the position sought are stated in these documents. They offer valuable clues as to the nature of the oral interview. For example, if the job involves supervisory responsibilities, the announcement will usually indicate that knowledge of modern supervisory methods and the qualifications of the candidate as a supervisor will be tested. If so, you can expect such questions, frequently in the form of a hypothetical situation which you are expected to solve. *Never* go into an oral without knowledge of the duties and responsibilities of the job you seek.

3. Think Through Each Qualification Required

   Try to visualize the kind of questions *you* would ask if you were a board member. How well could you answer them? Try especially to appraise your own knowledge and background in each area, *measured against the job sought,* and identify any areas in which you are weak. Be critical and realistic -- do not flatter yourself.

4. Do Some General Reading in Areas in Which You Feel You May be Weak

   For example, if the job involves supervision and your past experience has *not,* some general reading in supervisory methods and practices, particularly in the field of human relations, might be useful. *Do not* study agency procedures or detailed manuals. The oral board will be testing your understanding and capacity, *not* your memory.

5. Get a Good Night's Sleep and Watch Your General Health and Mental Attitude

   You will want a clear head at the interview. Take care of a cold or other minor ailment, and, of course, *no hangovers.*

D. WHAT TO DO THE DAY OF THE INTERVIEW

Now comes the day of the interview itself. Give yourself plenty of time to get there. Plan to arrive somewhat ahead of the scheduled time, particularly if your appointment is in the fore part of the day. If a previous candidate fails to appear, the board might be ready for you a bit early. By early afternoon an oral board is almost invariably behind schedule if there are many candidates, and you may have to wait. Take along a book or magazine to read, or your application to review. But leave any extraneous material in the waiting room when you go in for your interview. In any event, relax and compose yourself.

The matter of dress is important. The board is forming impressions about you -- from your experience, your manners, your attitudes, and from your appearance. Give your personal appearance careful attention. Dress your *best*, but not your flashiest. Choose conservative, appropriate clothing, and be sure it and you are immaculate. This is a business interview, and your appearance should indicate that you regard it as such. Besides, being well-groomed and properly dressed will help boost your confidence.

Sooner or later, someone will call your name and escort you into the interview room. *This is it.* From here on you are on your own. It is too late for any more preparation. But, remember, you asked for this opportunity to prove your fitness, and you are here because your request was granted.

E. WHAT HAPPENS WHEN YOU GO IN?

The usual sequence of events will be as follows: The clerk (who is often the board stenographer) will introduce you to the chairman of the oral board, who will introduce you to each other member of the board. Acknowledge the introductions before you sit down. Do not be surprised if you find a microphone facing you or a stenotypist sitting by. Oral interviews are usually recorded, in the event of an appeal or other review.

Usually the chairman of the board will open the interview by reviewing the highlights of your education and work experience from your application -- primarily for the benefit of the other members of the board, as well as to get the material into the record. Do not interrupt or comment unless there is an error or significant misinterpretation; if so, do not hesitate. But do not quibble about insignificant matters. Usually, also, he will ask you some question about your education, your experience, or your present job -- partly to get you started talking, to establish the interviewing "rapport." He may start the actual questioning, or turn it over to one of the other members. Frequently each member undertakes the questioning on a particular area, one in which he is perhaps most competent. So you can expect each member to participate in the examination. And because the time is limited, you may expect some rather abrupt switches in the direction the questioning takes. Do not be upset by it. Normally, a board member will not pursue a single line of questioning unless he discovers a particular strength or weakness.

After each member has participated, the chairman will usually ask whether any member has any further questions, then will ask you if you have anything you wish to add. Unless you are expecting this question, it may floor you. Or worse, it may start you off on an extended, extemporaneous speech. The board is not usually seeking more information. The question is principally to offer you a last opportunity to present further qualifications or to indicate that you have nothing to add. So, if you feel that a significant qualification or characteristic has been overlooked, it is proper to point it out in a sentence or so. Do not compliment the board on the thoroughness of their examination -- they have been sketchy, and you know it. If you wish, merely say, "No thank you, I have nothing further to add." This is a point where you can "talk yourself out" of a good impression or fail to present an important bit of information. *Remember, you close the interview yourself.*

The chairman will then say, "That is all, Mr. Smith, thank you." Do not be startled; the interview is over, and quicker than you think. Say, "Thank you and good morning," gather up your belongings and take your leave. Save your sigh of relief for the other side of the door.

F. HOW TO PUT YOUR BEST FOOT FORWARD

Throughout all this process, you may feel that the board individually and collectively is trying to pierce your defenses, to seek out your hidden weaknesses, and to embarrass and confuse you. Actually, this is not true. They are obliged to make an appraisal of your qualifications for the job you are seeking, and they *want to see you in your best light*. Remember, they must interview all **candidates** and a noncooperative candidate may become a failure in spite of their best efforts to bring out his qualifications. Here are fifteen(15) suggestions that will help you:

1. Be Natural. Keep Your Attitude Confident, But Not Cocky

If *you* are not confident that you can do the job, do not expect the *board* to be. Do not apologize for your weaknesses, try to bring out your strong points. The board is interested in a positive, not a negative presentation. Cockiness will antagonize any board member, and make him wonder if you are covering up a weakness by a false show of strength.

2. Get Comfortable, But Don't Lounge or Sprawl

Sit erectly but not stiffly. A careless posture may lead the board to conclude you are careless in other things, or at least that you are not impressed by the importance of the occasion to you. Either conclusion is natural, even if incorrect. Do not fuss with your clothing, or with a pencil or an ashtray. Your hands may occasionally be useful to emphasize a point; do not let them become a point of distraction.

3. Do Not Wisecrack or Make Small Talk

This is a serious situation, and your attitude should show that you consider it as such. Further, the time of the board is limited; they do not want to waste it, and neither should you.

4. Do Not Exaggerate Your Experience or Abilities

In the first place, from information in the application, from other interviews and other sources, the board may know more about you than you think; in the second place, you probably will not get away with it in the first place. An experienced board is rather adept at spotting such a situation. Do not take the chance.

5. If You Know a Member of the Board, Do Not Make a Point of It, Yet Do Not Hide It.

Certainly you are not fooling him, and probably not the other members of the board. Do not try to take advantage of your acquaintanceship -- it will probably do you little good.

6. Do Not Dominate the Interview

Let the board do that. They will give you the clues -- do not assume that you have to do all the talking. Realize that the board has a number of questions to ask you, and do not try to take up all the interview time by showing off your extensive knowledge of the answer to the first one.

15

7. Be Attentive

You only have twenty minutes or so, and you should keep your attention at its sharpest throughout. When a member is addressing a problem or a question to you, give him your undivided attention. Address your reply principally to him, but do not exclude the other members of the board.

8. Do Not Interrupt

A board member may be stating a problem for you to analyze. He will ask you a question when the time comes. Let him state the problem, and wait for the question.

9. Make Sure You Understand the Question

Do not try to answer until you are sure what the question is. If it is not clear, restate it in your own words or ask the board member to clarify it for you. But do not haggle about minor elements.

10. Reply Promptly But Not Hastily

A common entry on oral board rating sheets is "candidate responded readily," or "candidate hesitated in replies." Respond as promptly and quickly as you can, but do not jump to a hasty, ill-considered answer.

11. Do Not Be Peremptory in Your Answers

A brief answer is proper -- but do not fire your answer back. That is a losing game from your point of view. The board member can probably ask questions much faster than you can answer them.

12. Do Not Try To Create the Answer You Think the Board Member Wants

He is interested in what kind of mind you have and how it works -- not in playing games. Furthermore, he can usually spot this practice and will usually grade you down on it.

13. Do Not Switch Sides in Your Reply Merely to Agree With a Board Member

Frequently, a member will take a contrary position merely to draw you out and to see if you are willing and able to defend your point of view. Do not start a debate, yet do not surrender a good position. If a position is worth taking, it is worth defending.

] Do Not Be Afraid to Admit an Error in Judgment if You Are Shown to Be Wrong

The board knows that you are forced to reply without any opportunity for careful consideration. Your answer may be demonstrably wrong. If so, admit it and get on with the interview.

15. Do Not Dwell at Length on Your Present Job

The opening question may relate to your present assignment. Answer the question but do not go into an extended discussion. You are being examined for a *new* job, not your present one. As a matter of fact, try to phrase *all* your answers in terms of the job for which you are being examined.

G. BASIS OF RATING

Probably you will forget most of these "do's" and "don'ts" when you walk into the oral interview room. Even remembering them all will not insure you a passing grade. Perhaps you did not have the qualifications in the first place. But remembering them *will* help you to put your best foot forward, without treading on the toes of the board members.

Rumor and popular opinion to the contrary notwithstanding, an oral board wants you to make the best appearance possible. They know you are under pressure -- but they also want to see how you respond to it as a guide to what your reaction would be under the pressures of the job you seek. They will be influenced by the degree of poise you display, the personal traits you show, and the manner in which you respond.

EXAMINATION SECTION

EXAMINATION SECTION
TEST 1

DIRECTIONS: Each question or incomplete statement is followed by several suggested answers or completions. Select the one that BEST answers the question or completes the statement. *PRINT THE LETTER OF THE CORRECT ANSWER IN THE SPACE AT THE RIGHT.*

1. Upon arrival at the scene of an elevator pit fire, a ladder company captain discovers that there is a heavy smoke condition in a multi-car elevator shaft and that two people are trapped inside an elevator car. The captain decides to remove the trapped occupants via the elevator car's top escape hatch.
   In this situation, which action should the captain take?
   A. Have the trapped occupants removed to the roof of the disabled car, and then moved to the adjacent car via planks.
   B. Leave the power on to ensure that the safety brake remains engaged.
   C. Instruct three members secured with lifesaving ropes to operate from the car roof.
   D. Order one member to operate below the car to activate the safety brake.

   1.___

2. You are the captain of the first ladder company to arrive at a fire in a non-fireproof multiple dwelling at 2300 hours. Your unit must use its aerial ladder to remove three victims from the fire building.
   In performing this operation, you should
   A. have members ascend the ladder as it is being extended in order to prevent victims from climbing on to it
   B. insure that members assist each victim only as far as the turntable before ascending the ladder again
   C. assign the outside vent man to use the apparatus spotlight to pinpoint the victims' location and to reassure them
   D. designate the roofman to assist the OVM and the chauffeur in the rescue effort

   2.___

3. A captain supervising the rescue of a person by use of a portable or scaling ladder from a tower ladder basket must decide which ladder to utilize.
   Of the following factors, which one should he use as a guideline in making his decision?
   A. New aluminum scaling ladders are stronger than the older wooden models but are slightly heavier and harder to handle.
   B. Portable ladders provide more stability than scaling ladders when operated from the basket platform.

   3.___

C. More than one scaling ladder may be brought to the point of operations via the basket.

D. Using portable ladders eliminates the need to tie knots.

4. The captain of the first arriving engine company is ordered   4.___
   to take a standby position at an operation where several
   pounds of explosives have been found within a building.
   Which one of the following actions would be PROPER for
   the captain to order?
   A. Operate handie-talkies at a minimum of 100 feet from
      the site of the explosives.
   B. Remove sufficient hose from the pumper and snake it
      back and forth in front of the entrance to the
      building.
   C. Connect the pumper to a hydrant remote from the
      involved building and leave the pumps uncharged.
   D. Monitor the department radio from the chief's car,
      which should be parked at least 300 feet from the
      involved site.

5. When a heavy fire condition exists in a taxpayer building   5.___
   which has roof supports of lightweight open web steel
   joists, early roof collapse must be anticipated.
   Which one of the following statements concerning these
   roof joists is CORRECT?
   They
   A. will fail without warning and tend to *snap* when
      exposed to elevated temperatures
   B. must be coated with a cement fiber material which
      affords only a minimal fire resistance rating
   C. will be spaced from four to six feet apart when
      corrugated steel decking is used
   D. are spaced closer together than wood joists since
      the steel joists are lighter in weight

6. A captain conducting a unit drill on flat roof operations   6.___
   makes the following points to members during the drill:
   I. Firefighters operating on a roof should continuously
      be aware of an emergency escape route and should
      make certain that this route is available during the
      entire fire operation
   II. When members are cutting a roof vent opening over a
      top floor fire, fire exploding out of the opening
      may block their exit
   III. Members who receive a *direct* order to evacuate the
      roof area immediately should take the shortest way
      off the roof even if it is not necessarily the
      safest route

   Which one of the following choices lists only those
   remarks made by the captain that are generally CORRECT?
   A. I, II   B. I, III   C. II, III   D. I, II, III

7. At an emergency in a newly constructed high school which has physically handicapped non-ambulatory students in attendance, the captain of the first arriving unit decides to evacuate the building.
The captain should expect to find the fire drill and evacuation plan
    A. at the main entrance lobby
    B. at the fire command station
    C. in either the office of the assistant principal or the nurse's office
    D. in the offices of the principal and the custodian

7.___

8. You are the captain of the first arriving unit at a fire in an *ABR in process* school which has non-ambulatory students in attendance on the floor above the ground floor. In addition to the regular fire drills, an individualized safety plan is required for these children. You would be MOST likely to find each student's plan
    A. posted in the main lobby on the first floor
    B. posted at the fire command station
    C. on the apparatus of each first alarm unit
    D. in possession of the person in charge of the school

8.___

9. The captain of the first arriving unit at an incident involving transportation of hazardous materials transmits a 10-80 signal. The captain is unable to relate any further information concerning the materials in the truck because there are no placards or chemical names available. However, the captain is able to obtain the transporter's name and the license plate number and state.
It would be MOST appropriate for the captain to have this information given to the
    A. Incident Commander upon his arrival so that the transporter can be notified via the dispatcher
    B. Haz-Mat unit for notification of the transporter via cellular phone
    C. Police Department for a computer check on the owner who can identify the contents
    D. dispatcher who should notify the owner directly to obtain the identification of the product

9.___

10. At the scene of a valve alarm, the captain of the first arriving unit investigates the cause of alarm transmission. This investigation, completed before the arrival of the battalion chief, indicates that the alarm was transmitted because a sprinkler pipe had been accidentally broken by a hi-low.
In this situation, the captain should transmit radio signal 10-34
    A. Without Code   B. Code 1
    C. Code 2   D. Code 3

10.___

11. The captain of the first arriving unit at a fire scene   11.___
    must consider the effects of radiant heat on exposed
    surfaces.
    It would be APPROPRIATE for the captain to assume that
    radiant heat will
       A. not travel against the wind
       B. be scattered by smoke present in the atmosphere
       C. not travel long distances through air
       D. be emitted only in a direction perpendicular to the
          hot surface

12. Which one of the following methods should a captain direct 12.___
    his unit to employ in extinguishing a small sodium fire
    in a laboratory?
       A. Blanket the sodium with sodium carbonate.
       B. Immerse the sodium in a large bucket of water.
       C. Blanket the sodium with fluoroprotein foam.
       D. Immerse the sodium in sulfuric acid.

13. Assume that you are the captain of the first arriving   13.___
    ladder company at a first floor fire in a detached private
    dwelling with a peak roof.
    Of the following actions, it would be MOST appropriate
    for you to direct the
       A. roofman to make a rapid advance to search the second
          floor after the search of the first floor has been
          completed
       B. forcible entry man to force the main entrance door to
          give access to the interior stair for protection and
          control of this area
       C. can man to use the extinguisher to extinguish a fully
          involved room fire in order to prevent further
          extension
       D. OVM to perform outside ventilation of the first floor
          to permit the advance of the line

14. The captain of a ladder company at a top floor fire in a   14.___
    H-type building is supervising trench operations on the
    roof.
    It would be MOST appropriate for the captain to direct
    the members to
       A. cut the trench only after the main opening over the
          fire has been made
       B. avoid cutting any holes on the fire side of the trench
       C. raise two ladders to the roof of the building to
          ensure safe egress for members cutting the trench
       D. avoid the use of glass skylights as stop points for
          the trench

15. Members are removing occupants from the fifth floor of a   15.___
    fire building via a tower ladder basket with double-acting
    swinging gates.
    It would be MOST appropriate for the captain supervising
    this operation to order

A. the occupants to be removed directly to the street if the basket is needed for additional rescues
B. the apparatus to be placed perpendicular to the building to shorten the basket travel distance and to reduce time required to reach the occupants
C. that an angular approach of the basket be used to permit ease in entering or alighting from the basket
D. that the basket be elevated to a point where its middle railing is level with the middle of the window, enabling occupants to step easily into the basket

16. A captain is directing ventilation operations on the floor above the fire floor at a school which is in compliance with the 1968 Building Code.
In this situation, the captain would be CORRECT in assuming that the school's corridors are subdivided by smoke barriers into maximum lengths of _____ feet.
   A. 50   B. 100   C. 150   D. 300   16.___

17. A captain performing a tour of duty on a fireboat responds to the scene of a collision between a Department of Sanitation scow and a pier. While planning a course of action, the captain realizes that the scow should remain afloat to a draft of 12 feet, or until the catwalk around the hopper is barely above water.
He should conclude that this will be TRUE
   A. even if both the shell plating and the bulkheads of the hopper are ruptured
   B. even if the shell plating of the hopper is ruptured, as long as the bulkheads are watertight
   C. even if the bulkheads are ruptured, as long as the shell plating of the hopper is watertight
   D. only if the bulkheads and the shell plating of the hopper are both watertight

17.___

18. A captain of an engine company is special-called to the scene of a vehicle fire. Upon arrival, he finds a fire in a pickup truck and notices that there is a propane fuel decal displayed on the left rear bumper of the truck.
The captain orders the members to stay clear of the propane tank's relief valve discharge point, which must be located within _____ degrees of the _____, pointing

18.___

_____.
   A. 15; vertical; upward   B. 15; horizontal; downward
   C. 45; horizontal; upward   D. 45; vertical; downward

19. The captain of the first ladder company to arrive at a fire in an unsprinklered two-story factory which employs 50 people on the second floor decides to evacuate the building.
Of the following, which is the provision of the Labor Law which should guide the captain in making his decision?

19.___

    A. No fire alarm signal system is required because there
       are only 50 people employed on the second floor.
    B. A fire alarm signal system is required because there
       are more than 25 people employed on the second floor.
    C. No fire alarm signal system is required because the
       building is only two stories high.
    D. A fire alarm signal system is required because the
       building is two stories high.

20. You are the captain of the first arriving engine company   20.___
at a fire in a three-story fireproof factory building
erected in 1911. The building has a medium hazard occupancy on the first two floors and a high hazard occupancy
on the third floor.
You should expect to find a sprinkler system on
    A. all three floors
    B. the third floor only
    C. none of the floors since the building is fireproof
    D. none of the floors since the building was erected
       prior to 1913

21. A captain is supervising two members administering CPR to   21.___
a middle-aged woman who has collapsed on the street in
front of quarters.
During this procedure, the captain should make certain
that
    A. members compress the tip of the lower sternum no more
       than 2 inches since this tip can be pressed into the
       kidneys and cause damage
    B. members compress the victim's sternum to a depth of
       1 to 1½ inches for proper CPR
    C. any interruption of CPR is for a maximum of 15 seconds
    D. members' fingers do not rest on the ribs of the
       victim during the compression phase

22. A captain in command of a unit is assigned to remove a   22.___
body from the scene of a fatal fire where both canvas
and plastic body bags are available.
During this operation, the captain should instruct
members to
    A. place the canvas body bag inside of the plastic body
       bag before moving the victim to the ambulance
    B. remove the outer body bag after the victim has been
       placed inside the ambulance
    C. retrieve the outer body bag after the victim has been
       transported to the morgue
    D. retrieve the inner body bag after the victim has been
       transported to the morgue

23. A captain arrives at the scene of an emergency and   23.___
witnesses a person suffering a Grand Mal epileptic
seizure. The captain orders that a rolled handkerchief
be placed between the victim's side teeth while the
victim is kept lying down.
The captain's action is

A. *correct*
B. *incorrect*, mainly because the victim should be kept in a sitting position
C. *incorrect*, mainly because a solid object such as a spoon or piece of wood should be placed in the victim's mouth
D. *incorrect*, mainly because a rolled handkerchief should be used only if the victim is suffering a Petit Mal seizure

24. During the overhaul phase of a fire in a concrete building   24.___
    which is under construction, a captain notices protruding
    cables, coils of tendons and anchors.
    These findings should lead the captain to conclude that
    this type of construction is _____ concrete.
    A. post-tensioned   B. pre-tensioned
    C. precast   D. conventional reinforced

25. A captain is supervising members breaching a brick   25.___
    exterior wall from the basket of a tower ladder.
    Of the following, in this situation, it would be MOST
    appropriate for the captain to have
    A. the brick cut in a rectangular form large enough so
       that the power saw can be inserted into the opening
       to cut the inner wall
    B. a pneumatic hammer used to cut the brick in a trian-
       gular form with the vertex angle upward to help
       prevent collapse of the brickwork
    C. the first cut with the power saw made at the mortar
       joint since this is the easiest cut and will loosen
       the bricks
    D. a pneumatic hammer used to cut the brick in a trian-
       gular form with the vertex angle downward to prevent
       collapse of the brickwork

26. A captain is supervising overhauling operations in a peak   26.___
    roof private dwelling.
    Of the following actions, it would be MOST appropriate
    for the captain to direct his unit to
    A. make the initial opening below a hot spot in a wall
       to prevent fire from lapping into the room
    B. start at the center when removing one-piece base-
       boards because mitered corners make removal of the
       baseboards difficult
    C. cut roof boards from above because it is easier than
       attempting to push them out from the interior
    D. begin extensive removal of roof boards to insure
       complete extinguishment of fire between the roof
       boards and outer covering

27. A captain's unit is special called to deliver a foam   27.____
    carrier and Angus foam cannon to a flammable liquid fire.
    Upon arriving at the scene, the captain is ordered to
    place the foam cannon into operation.
    Of the following, it would be MOST appropriate for the
    captain to order his firefighters to
    A. supply 1 3/4" hose with appropriate fittings to the
       foam cannon since high water pressure and low water
       volume is needed to produce efficient foam
    B. connect a 2½" hose line to an inlet on one side of
       the cannon and then connect a line to the other side
       only if more water volume is necessary
    C. shut down the water supply or significantly reduce
       the pressure if repositioning of the foam cannon
       becomes necessary
    D. use the foam cannon controls to regulate the water
       flow and pressure for more accurate reach and volume

28. A captain is ordering rope to be used for speedy and   28.____
    efficient stretching of hose lines to upper floors and
    roofs.
    What is the MOST appropriate type and length of rope for
    the captain to order?
    A. 50 feet of 13/16 inch manila
    B. 75 feet of 3/8 inch nylon
    C. 50 feet of 3/8 inch nylon
    D. 75 feet of 9/16 inch manila

29. At a fire in a mobile home, an engine company captain,   29.____
    whose unit is first to arrive at the scene, should order
    his company to stretch
    A. 1 3/4" hose with an automatic fog tip because it is
       more maneuverable than larger size hose
    B. 1 3/4" hose with a solid stream tip because of the
       physical layout of a mobile home
    C. 2½" hose with an automatic fog tip because coverage
       would be greatly increased, thereby reducing the
       total water damage
    D. 2½" hose with a solid stream tip because a larger
       volume of water is needed quickly in a mobile home
       fire

30. Which one of the following situations should a captain   30.____
    recognize as a possible indication of arson?
    A. Furniture found in a commercial occupancy reported
       to have been vacant
    B. A motor vehicle fire where the owner or driver is not
       present to account for the fire
    C. A clean or unburned area under stock or furniture in
       an industrial occupancy
    D. Burning and charring in an upward and outward direc-
       tion at an apartment fire

31. The captain, while supervising overhauling activities at   31.____
a suspected arson fire, detects an odor similar to wet
matchheads.
It would be MOST appropriate for the captain to suspect
that this odor was the result of burning
    A. phosphorous   B. hydrocyanic acid gas
    C. carbon disulfide   D. sulfur candles

32. The chief in charge of a suspicious fire orders the   32.____
ladder company captain to collect and preserve a 1 inch x
14 inch piece of wood flooring as evidence. As the chief
is leaving the scene, he gives the captain a large plastic
bag and a new, unused 10-inch high, one-gallon metal can
with a lid.
In order to properly preserve the evidence, the captain
should
    A. leave the flooring intact and place it in the plastic
       bag
    B. cut the flooring and place it into the can with the
       lid put on loosely
    C. leave the flooring intact, place it into the can,
       and then place the can inside the plastic bag
    D. cut the flooring and place it into the can with the
       lid put on tight

33. When the owner-occupant fails to vacate a building within   33.____
the stipulated time after the receipt of a vacate order,
the captain should
    A. forward an A-8 to the Department of Buildings
    B. forward a special report to the Chief of Operations
    C. issue a summons to the owner-occupant at the premises
    D. notify the dispatcher for priority fire marshal
       response

34. While you are making an inspection of a borough communica-   34.____
tion office which is undergoing extensive reconstruction
by outside contractors, the borough chief fire alarm
dispatcher asks you how frequently the office will be
reinspected.
As the captain, you should answer that the building will
be reinspected
    A. daily   B. weekly   C. biweekly   D. monthly

35. During a 9x6 tour, an engine company captain responds to   35.____
a helicopter staging area during external load operations.
Of the following, what fire protection equipment should
the captain expect to find at the staging area?
Two _____ extinguishers.
    A. 2½ gallon water-type
    B. 20 lb. dry chemical multi-purpose
    C. 2½ gallon AFFF
    D. 15 lb. CO_2

36. The captain of a ladder company is operating at the scene   36.____
of a fire on the third floor of a Class A multiple dwelling which has triplex apartments throughout the building.
The roofman operating above the fire informs the captain
via handie-talkie that there are doors in the hallway with
no numerical designation on them.
Of the following, it would be MOST appropriate for the
captain to inform the roofman that these doors are the
  A. second exits from the apartments below and that they
     serve two apartments simultaneously
  B. main entrance doors to upper floor apartments in the
     building
  C. second exits from apartments and it is difficult to
     tell which apartments they serve
  D. main entrance doors to lower floor apartments in the
     building

37. At an incinerator operation, the roofman of a ladder   37.____
company informs the captain, via the handie-talkie, that
it is necessary to force the door to the fly ash collector and clear the blockage at the top of the incinerator
chute.
Of the following, it would be MOST appropriate for the
captain to order the roofman to _____ the blockage in
the chute.
  A. await the arrival of the building maintenance staff
     so that they can clear
  B. proceed to force the fly ash collector door and clear
  C. await the arrival of the forcible entry team to assist
     with forcing the door and clearing
  D. proceed to force the fly ash collector door, but
     wait for the building maintenance staff to clear

38. The captain of the first ladder company to arrive at the   38.____
scene of a reported fire in a 25-story fireproof sliver
building receives a report via handie-talkie from the OVM
that there are smoke and flames showing on the 15th floor
in the rear of the building.
Of the following, who should the captain send to search
the floor above the fire?
The
  A. roofman
  B. outside vent man and the chauffeur   *
  C. roofman and outside vent man
  D. outside vent man

39. A captain must determine the appropriate number of hose   39.____
lengths and the method of loading hose which are best
suited for his unit's apparatus.
In doing this, the captain must consult with the
  A. captains of adjoining units *only*
  B. captains of adjoining units and the battalion commander
  C. captains of adjoining units and the division commander
  D. battalion commander and the division commander

40. The captain of a ladder company at a vacant building fire   40.___
    takes the following precautions:
    I. Assigns two members, one of whom is equipped with a
       handie-talkie, to search all floors below the
       operating force for the presence of other fires
    II. Checks the ceilings in the apartment below the fire
        to alert members above of holes in the path of their
        advance
    III. Secures bulkhead doors, skylights, and scuttle
         covers before taking up to facilitate future opera-
         tions in the building
    The captain is CORRECT in taking which of the above actions?
       A. I, II   B. I, III   C. II, III   D. I, II, III

————

KEY (CORRECT ANSWERS)

1. A	11. B	21. D	31. A
2. C	12. A	22. B	32. D
3. C	13. B	23. A	33. C
4. D	14. C	24. A	34. B
5. C	15. C	25. B	35. B
6. A	16. D	26. D	36. C
7. D	17. D	27. C	37. B
8. D	18. A	28. B	38. B
9. C	19. C	29. A	39. D
10. A	20. A	30. B	40. A

————

TEST 2

DIRECTIONS: Each question or incomplete statement is followed by several suggested answers or completions. Select the one that BEST answers the question or completes the statement. *PRINT THE LETTER OF THE CORRECT ANSWER IN THE SPACE AT THE RIGHT.*

1. The captain of an engine company which is the only unit at   1.___
   the scene of a manhole fire considers taking the following
   safety precautions prior to the arrival of electric
   company personnel:
     I. Establishing a safety zone around the involved man-
        hole and adjacent manholes
    II. Checking the fuse service panel in adjacent buildings
        for the presence of heat
   III. Using a fog stream to let water flow into the manhole
        to prevent destructive distillation of cables

   Of the following choices, which one lists the precautions
   the captain should take in the above situation?
     A. I, III   B. II, III   C. I, II   D. I, II, III

2. A captain conducting a regularly scheduled theatre   2.___
   inspection observes several violations that cannot be
   corrected prior to the next live performance.
   In this situation, the captain must IMMEDIATELY notify the
     A. Bureau of Fire Prevention
     B. battalion chief on duty
     C. deputy chief on duty
     D. city-wide command chief

3. A captain observes kerosene space heaters being sold in   3.___
   a hardware store. He notices that there is no sign posted
   near the heaters and there are no tags attached to the
   heaters to inform the public that the use or storage of
   kerosene heaters is prohibited in the city.
   In this situation, the captain should
     A. forward an A-8 to the Bureau of Fire Prevention and
        issue a forthwith violation order
     B. issue a summons
     C. forward an A-8 to the Bureau of Fire Prevention and
        telephone the Department of Consumer Affairs
     D. issue a forthwith violation order

4. During AFID, the captain questions firefighters about the   4.___
   field inspection card.
   Which one of the following statements made by the firefighters should the captain point out as being CORRECT?
     A. Fire Department policy requires that a card must
        be maintained for all commercial and and residential
        premises.

B. When a fatal fire occurs in a building, the victims
   must be listed in red ink on the rear of the card.
C. When a building is demolished, the word *demolished*
   must be written in red ink diagonally across the face
   of the card and the card retained for 6 years.
D. If a building has been identified for the critical
   information dispatch system, the notation *CIDS* must
   be marked on the top of the card.

5. A company is in quarters just before going out on AFID.   5.___
   The captain is reviewing, with the members, the codes and
   department guidelines pertinent to the premises they will
   be inspecting.
   The captain should point out each of the following EXCEPT:
   A. Underground Transit Authority leased commercial
      occupancies must be scheduled for annual inspection
   B. *Requested Inspection* has priority since it is critical
      to the immediate correction of life-threatening
      hazard
   C. A multi-story U.S. post office building which employs
      several hundred people over a 24-hour per day opera-
      tion is a code *B* post office
   D. CIDS information on imminently hazardous conditions
      can be entered immediately into the CIDS program by
      requesting the staff officer on duty to telephone
      the CADO unit

6. Assume that you are a captain and blasting operations have   6.___
   been suspended at a construction site within your administrative district. You then make a terminal inspection of
   the site.
   According to fire prevention directives, to assure that
   the magazine remains empty while blasting operations are
   suspended, you should make certain that _____ until
   operations resume.
   A. one inspection is made each week during the 6x9 tour
   B. one inspection is made each month during the 9x6 tour
   C. two inspections are made each week at irregular hours
   D. two inspections are made each month when the watchman
      is on duty

7. A captain is supervising the inspection of an explosives   7.___
   magazine located in his district. A permit has been issued
   for above ground blasting at a site where a building is
   being erected.
   The captain should remind the individuals concerned that,
   unless a special permit has been granted by the commissioner, above ground blasting can ONLY be conducted Monday
   through _____ between _____.
   A. Friday; 7 A.M. and 7 P.M.
   B. Friday; 8 A.M. and 6 P.M.
   C. Saturday; 7 A.M. and 7 P.M.
   D. Saturday; 8 A.M. and 6 P.M.

8. The hydrant officer of your unit, a newly assigned   8.___
   lieutenant, informs you that he has taken the following
   actions:
   I. When it was discovered on inspection that a hydrant's
      defective gland box had not been repaired since the
      last semi-annual inspection period, he submitted a
      new Defective Hydrant Report (CD-63)
   II. When a second hydrant card (BF-47) was started, he
      discarded the old defective hydrant forms and hydrant
      repair work tickets associated with the first hydrant
      card
   III. Upon receiving a repaired hydrant work ticket, he
      reinspected the unserviceable hydrant and found the
      same defects; he then telephoned the repair yard to
      resolve the problem

   Of the following choices, which one includes only those
   of the lieutenant's actions that you, as the company
   commander, should approve?
      A. I, II   B. II, III   C. I, III   D. I, II, III

9. A captain overhears the following remarks made by a group   9.___
   of firefighters discussing hydrant inspection duty:
   I. A blue disc indicates the hydrant is defective but
      can be used for firefighting
   II. A lime yellow disc on parkway hydrants indicates
      the curb valve is shut down
   III. A plugged hydrant is inspected annually and the words
      Plugged Hydrant in red are placed at the top of the
      Hydrant Inspection Card

   Of these statements, the captain should tell the firefighters that the INCORRECT ones are:
      A. I, II   B. I, III   C. II, III   D. I, II, III

10. Upon returning to quarters from a structural fire, the   10.___
    captain orders members to inspect the Scott 4.5 masks.
    As the captain supervises the inspections, he notes the
    procedures being used.
    Of the following procedures, which one must the captain
    make sure members use in the inspection of the masks?
       A. The high pressure hose coupling is uncoupled from the
          cylinder and the hose coupling is checked for cracks.
       B. The metal shield over the pressure reducer assembly
          is checked to insure that it is not loose and that it
          is held secure by the two screws and clips on each
          side.
       C. All *E* clips are checked to insure that they are
          attached to the facepiece, with the openings facing
          away from the demand regulator opening.
       D. The facepiece is submersed in a solution of two
          tablespoons of chlorine bleach and one gallon of
          water for five minutes.

11. As the captain of an engine company supervising a hose   11.___
    test, which one of the following actions should you
    order members to perform?
    A. Stretch a maximum of three lengths of hose for each
       hose test.
    B. Lash the hose to a discharge outlet on the pump
       operator's side of the apparatus.
    C. Fit the hose with an open nozzle and lash the hose
       to a substantial object.
    D. Have pump pressure maintained for 30 seconds at
       250 psi.

12. A captain supervising the maintenance of handie-talkies   12.___
    is explaining various features of the MX-330 and the
    HT-220 handie-talkies to members.
    Which one of the following statements should the captain
    make?
    A. HT-220 must be charged every 8 hours.
    B. MX-330 battery capacity is about 8 hours.
    C. HT-220 is equipped with a *time out timer*.
    D. MX-330 is preferred in feedback assisted rescue.

13. Captains are mandated by department rules and regulations   13.___
    to have firefighters in their respective units check,
    operate, and inspect certain firefighting equipment every
    Monday during the 9x6 tour.
    Which one of the following choices lists the equipment
    that must be operated or inspected during this tour?
    A. Lifesaving rope, masks, handie-talkie, reserve
       apparatus
    B. Lifesaving rope, resuscitators, survey meters, spare
       apparatus
    C. Life belts, hurst tool, portable electrical generator,
       hand holds, and rails
    D. Life belts, emergency electrical power generator,
       bulk foam storage tank, seat belts

14. The commanding officer of a unit, when advised of a   14.___
    complaint of discrimination by a firefighter, should
    A. have the firefighter make an immediate notification
       to the office of the inspector general regarding the
       alleged discrimination
    B. investigate and resolve the complaint or take required
       corrective action
    C. contact the Equal Employment Opportunity Unit to
       register the complaint
    D. forward a report of the alleged discrimination to the
       office of the fire commissioner

15. At the change of tours, a captain is discussing the   15.___
    department's policy on situational stress and substance
    abuse with the incoming lieutenant.
    Which one of the following points should the captain make?

A. If a member is referred to the counseling service unit by an officer, the member's compliance or non-compliance with treatment will be reported to the referring officer.
B. When members are referred to a psychiatrist for an evaluation/consultation for a duty status determination, the cost will be borne by the individual.
C. If a member who is diagnosed as being mentally ill refuses to cooperate with recommended treatment, he should be referred to the Bureau of Health Services for appropriate action.
D. If a member who is a substance abuser refuses to comply with recommended treatment, he should be referred to the Bureau of Fire Investigation.

16. A unit commander would be acting PROPERLY if he institutes non-judicial disciplinary proceedings when a member of his command has
    A. refused to clean the bathroom when ordered by his lieutenant
    B. been AWOL for 12 hours of a 6x9 tour
    C. readily admitted guilt of a flagrant violation of regulations
    D. declined to accept non-judicial proceedings

16.___

17. A captain has found it necessary to prefer charges against a member of his unit.
Unless delayed due to unusual conditions, department regulations require that charges be forwarded to the office of the inspector general with all endorsements within _____ after the occurrence.
    A. 48 hours   B. 6 days   C. 10 days   D. 15 days

17.___

18. Which one of the following points should a captain stress in the preparation of a company drill on incinerator equipment?
    A. Extension of a fire in an incinerator is more common than in a compactor since the incinerator is designed for burning.
    B. Smoke emitting from a chute door is an indication that the blockage is generally below that floor.
    C. An acceptable method of freeing chute blockages is to tie a rope to a cinder block and drop the block from above.
    D. It is preferred that material causing a blockage be burned off in the chute because it is designed to withstand the same heat as the fire box.

18.___

19. As the captain of the second arriving unit at the scene of a fire, you are informed by the lieutenant of the first arriving engine company that the degree of outward distortion in the walls has raised the possibility of a collapse.

19.___

Of the following conditions reported to you by the lieutenant, which one should you rule out as a factor in
determining the extent of wall distortion?
    A. Thickness of the wall
    B. Temperature difference between the top and bottom
       portions of the wall
    C. Height of the wall and distance between supports
    D. Coefficient of expansion of the materials of the wall

20. Which one of the following statements would be MOST
    appropriate for a captain to include in a drill con-
    cerning hazardous materials?   20.___
    A. Shipping containers for poisons have pressure relief
       devices and probably will not *bleve* under fire
       conditions.
    B. The products of combustion of poisons are always more
       hazardous than the poison itself.
    C. Poison containers can be considered safe once they
       have been emptied.
    D. It may be less dangerous to allow a poison to be
       consumed in a fire than to extinguish the fire.

21. A captain enters quarters early for a 6x9 tour and   21.___
    observes the lieutenant working the 9x6 tour conducting
    a critique of a brownstone fire from which the unit has
    just returned.
    Which one of the statements made by the lieutenant
    concerning ventilation at these buildings should the
    captain recognize as being CORRECT?
    A. If the outside vent man is needed to assist the
       chauffeur in front of the building and the fire is
       in the rear of the first floor, the roofman should
       perform outside ventilation of the fire area before
       proceeding to the roof.
    B. In order to ensure rapid ventilation of the building,
       the roofman should use the adjoining building as the
       primary means of access to the roof.
    C. If the closet door leading to the scuttle ladder is
       closed, the roofman should descend the scuttle
       ladder in order to properly ventilate the top floor.
    D. The roofman should ventilate the roof of the adjoin-
       ing building when heat and smoke may be expected to
       spread to the adjoining building.

22. During a critique of operations which occurred in a fire- 22.___
    proof hotel, a member states that standpipe hose was
    located in a locked metal cabinet on the main floor near
    the standpipe riser instead of being stored in racks on
    each floor.
    In response to this remark, the captain should explain
    that, according to the Building Code, this condition is
    A. *illegal*, since the cabinet must be unlocked
    B. *legal*, if required equipment is maintained and a sign
       is located in each stair enclosure on the main floor
       stating clearly where the storage cabinet is located

C. *illegal*, since standpipe hose may be omitted from racks in J-2 occupancies only

D. *legal*, if required equipment is maintained and a sign is located in each stair enclosure on every floor stating clearly where the storage cabinet is located

23. Upon returning to quarters from a fire in a high-rise office building where elevator problems were encountered, the captain decides to conduct a critique regarding the use of elevators in the operational phase.
Which one of the following points would be MOST appropriate for the captain to make during the critique?

A. Once the *Fireman Service* switch in the car is activated, only the street lobby keyed switch can override it.

B. Remove the key from the elevator car keyed switch, and leave the switch in the *Fireman Service* position to prevent unauthorized use of a *Fireman Service* elevator.

C. Operating the *Call Cancel* button will cause the elevator car to stop at the next available floor landing and the doors will remain closed.

D. The *Call Cancel* button must be pressed whenever entering a car on *Normal* service in order to clear the floor selection panel.

23.___

24. Company commanders must ensure that 5-gallon cans of fluoroprotein foam are carried by each engine and ladder company.
These cans of foam are required to be replaced with full cans when they are LESS than _____ full.
A. 1/4   B. 1/2   C. 2/3   D. 3/4

24.___

25. You are a captain and your apparatus has been involved in a major accident.
You would be justified in moving the apparatus before the arrival of the safety operating battalion or photo unit when the accident has resulted in

A. a narrow city street being blocked during rush hour

B. one lane of a city street being blocked during heavy rush hour traffic

C. one lane of an express highway being blocked during light, fast-moving traffic conditions

D. one lane of an express highway being blocked during heavy rush hour traffic

25.___

26. An engine company captain is reviewing the firehouse emergency action plan with his company safety officer.
The captain makes the following statements:

I. One copy of the plan shall be posted in a prominent place and be available for review by all members

II. A second copy of the plan shall be filed with the safety bulletins in the company office and be available for inspection by New York State OSHA inspectors.

26.___

III. An entry shall be made in the company journal each time the officer on duty reviews the plan with members

IV. Questions or inquiries for information about the escape plan shall be directed to the battalion safety officer

Which of the following lists ONLY those statements which are CORRECT?
A. II, III, IV
B. I, II, III
C. I, II, IV
D. I, III, IV

27. During a multi-unit drill, a captain orders his unit to hoist a portable ladder to the roof of a four-story building.
Which one of the following is an APPROPRIATE instruction for the captain to give during this evolution?
A. Insert the rope above the rung marked with a single piece of one-inch tape.
B. Position the tip of the ladder between the rope and the building throughout the hoisting operation.
C. Affix the rope to the ladder while the ladder is leaning against the building in a nearly vertical position.
D. Tie a clove hitch and binder on the rung marked with two pieces of one-inch tape.

27.___

28. A captain is conducting a drill on procedures to be followed at subway fires and emergencies.
Which one of the following should the captain describe as a CORRECT action to be taken at these operations?
A. A solid stream nozzle must be used since a fog nozzle will generate excessive heat in a subway tunnel.
B. Ladder company members conducting searches should always work in pairs and have at least one radio per pair.
C. Metal tools should never be carried into a subway tunnel because of the danger of electrocution associated with the third rail.
D. At a train derailment, when penetration of the skin of the car with power tools is necessary, it is best to cut at an area where there are rows of rivets.

28.___

29. A captain's unit is participating in a drill on the safety precautions taken by the high rise roof team (HRRT) during helicopter operations. Following are three actions which the captain as the HRRT officer might perform during the drill:
I. Approach the helicopter after receiving the signal from the pilot and position himself alongside the helicopter at the rear of the compartment door
II. Control the approach of members, supervise loading and unloading and monitor handie-talkie during flight
III. Board the helicopter first, leave the helicopter last, and select an assembly area near a roof bulkhead away from the landing area

29.___

Of the following choices, which one includes only those actions which the captain should take during the drill?
   A. I, II   B. I, III   C. II, III   D. I, II, III

30. At a company drill, a captain orders his firefighters to set up the Akron New Yorker multiversal nozzle in the portable position.
Of the following actions, members would be CORRECT if they
   A. placed the multiversal in the portable ground base with the two inlets in the siamese facing directly to the front and in line with the front leg of the portable ground base
   B. secured the multiversal with the lifesaving rope to prevent backward movement
   C. connected the hose lines to the siamese before the required knots were tied
   D. supplied the multiversal with two hose lines brought straight back for a distance of 15 feet from the siamese before making bends and turns in the hose

31. A lieutenant preparing a CD-72 for a firefighter who has suffered a broken leg asks the captain when an entry must be made on the DOSH-400 form.
The captain should state that the entry must be made within _____ days.
   A. 6   B. 10   C. 14   D. 30

32. Which one of the following statements concerning the MX-330 handie-talkie is CORRECT?
   A. The voice quality is equal to the old HT-220 model, but the MX-330 eliminates the stuck button problem.
   B. When the light on the top of the set comes on, the battery should be changed.
   C. The squelch control button should be adjusted to a position just past the quieting point to enable the set to achieve its best reception.
   D. All assigned handie-talkies should be charged at the beginning of each tour and immediately after being received in exchange from Division Depot.

33. The captain of an engine company equipped with an aluminum extension ladder instructs a lieutenant to make up a control sheet to ensure proper maintenance of the ladder.
Which one of the following procedures should the captain make certain that the lieutenant includes on the control sheet?
_____ shall be applied to all contacting surfaces _____.
   A. Paste wax; monthly
   B. Paraffin; every three months
   C. Light oil; every six months
   D. Candle wax; annually

30.___

31.___

32.___

33.___

34. All performance evaluation reports for Firefighters 1st,   34.___
2nd, and 3rd grade are to be reviewed and signed by the
commanding officer.
In the event of a long-term absence of the commanding
officer, when a detailed captain is assigned to fill the
long-term vacancy, the
    A. detailed captain must review and sign the evaluations
       and forward the reports to the Division Commander
    B. senior regularly assigned lieutenant must review the
       evaluations and forward the reports to the Evaluation
       Desk, Bureau of Personnel
    C. detailed captain must review and sign the evaluations
       and forward the reports to the Evaluation Desk,
       Bureau of Personnel
    D. senior regularly assigned lieutenant must review and
       sign the evaluations and forward the reports to the
       Division Commander

35. The captain of an engine company has a problem interpret-   35.___
ing a paragraph on a department order.
To obtain a proper interpretation of this order, of the
following, it would be MOST appropriate for the captain to
    A. telephone the Notification Desk, Bureau of Operations
    B. apply to the Bureau of Personnel through the chain
       of command
    C. telephone the Borough Command office
    D. apply to the office of the fire commissioner through
       the chain of command

36. As a captain, you are responsible for the disbursement of   36.___
funds from the firehouse special expense fund.
In performing this task, you must limit expenditures to
_____ per purchase and keep a record of all transactions
_____.
    A. $20; in the office record journal
    B. $25; in an inexpensive copy book
    C. $20; on an FS-1 form
    D. $25; in the office record journal

37. A relocated engine company is operating at a 10-26 in a   37.___
fireproof multiple dwelling. The occupant of the fire
apartment informs the engine company captain that the
owner of the building has not installed the required
smoke detector.
In this situation, it would be MOST appropriate for the
captain to
    A. refer the occupant to the Department of Housing
       Preservation and Development
    B. telephone the information to the Bureau of Fire
       Prevention upon return to quarters
    C. forward an A-8B fire department referral report
    D. inform the administrative company to forward an
       A-8B fire department referral report

38. For a 10-26 where only one engine company commanded by a lieutenant and one ladder company commanded by a captain are operating and no chief responds, a fire report or delayed report memo must be forwarded by the _____ officer within _____.
    A. engine; 72 hours
    B. ladder; 72 hours
    C. engine; 1 week
    D. ladder; 1 week

    38.____

39. A captain reviewing the particulars of a two-month-old line-of-duty injury suffered by a member finds it necessary to examine the company journal entry which was made at the time the injury occurred.
    To assist him in locating this entry quickly, he should check the flagging column for the code letters
    A. Inj   B. LOD   C. ML   D. SL

    39.____

40. A captain selecting members to attend chauffeur training school must ensure that the selected members
    A. be chosen on the basis of driving ability or seniority
    B. have been given at least 10 hours of driver training prior to attending chauffeur school
    C. have been trained in separate half hour segments excluding emergency responses prior to attending chauffeur school
    D. be chosen on the basis of seniority in the company in which they are serving

    40.____

KEY (CORRECT ANSWERS)

1. C	11. D	21. D	31. A
2. B	12. B	22. B	32. D
3. C	13. A	23. C	33. B
4. D	14. B	24. A	34. A
5. B	15. A	25. C	35. B
6. C	16. B	26. B	36. B
7. C	17. B	27. C	37. C
8. C	18. C	28. B	38. D
9. D	19. B	29. A	39. A
10. D	20. D	30. D	40. C

EXAMINATION SECTION
TEST 1

DIRECTIONS: Each question or incomplete statement is followed by several suggested answers or completions. Select the one that BEST answers the question or completes the statement. *PRINT THE LETTER OF THE CORRECT ANSWER IN THE SPACE AT THE RIGHT.*

1. A captain is in command of an operation involving a small fire in a vehicle on an express highway at 0300 hours on a cold winter morning.
   Of the following actions, it would generally be APPROPRIATE for the captain to
   A. avoid the use of salt or sand on run-off water during freezing conditions
   B. order that the furthest flares be placed 250 feet from the scene if he estimates the fastest traffic speed at 50 MPH
   C. conduct operations across the center divider to minimize traffic disruption and danger from *rubber-necking* drivers
   D. order members to move the vehicle and apparatus off the roadway to a safe location for necessary examination and overhaul

   1.___

2. A ladder company captain is conducting a drill on the proper method for a member to use when descending an aerial ladder with an ambulatory victim.
   The captain should point out that the member should
   A. place himself two rungs below the rung on which the victim is standing and descend in unison with the victim
   B. have the victim grasp the beams when descending at a steep angle to facilitate control of the victim
   C. encourage the victim to look down quickly during the descent so that he will know they are making progress
   D. use his body to press the victim against the ladder if the victim panics

   2.___

3. A captain is supervising the removal of a victim from the upper floor of a building via a Stokes stretcher in a tower ladder basket. The captain takes the following actions:
   I. Informs members that smooth basket operation is imperative when they are descending with the Stokes stretcher
   II. Instructs a member to lash the Stokes stretcher to the top railing of the basket
   III. Directs the basketman to perform the lowering operation

   3.___

Which one of the following choices lists only those actions taken by the captain which are CORRECT?
  A. I, II   B. I, III   C. II, III   D. I, II, III

4. A company officer responds to an oil burner fire in the cellar of a 33-story fireproof apartment building built in 1972. He orders the firefighter to take the following actions:
      I. Shut down the power to the oil burner by using the emergency remote control switch located outside the entrance leading to the boiler room
     II. Shut down the oil supply line valve at the oil burner unit
    III. Use an extinguisher with aqueous film forming foam to extinguish fire in the pit

    The officer's handling of this situation is
      A. *correct*
      B. *incorrect*, mainly because the emergency remote control switch will be found at the top of the cellar stairs
      C. *incorrect*, mainly because the oil supply line valve will be found only at the oil storage tank
      D. *incorrect*, mainly because fluoroprotein foam is the only foam that should be used in this situation

4.___

5. Which one of the following factors does NOT influence the severity of a backdraft?
    The
      A. temperature, pressure, and type of gases involved
      B. size and location of the fire area
      C. type and size of the opening made by the fire department
      D. amount of heat generated when an opening is made

5.___

6. The captain of the first due engine company arrives at an emergency in a high-rise building. The emergency on the 52nd floor involves a transformer which has a *polychlorinated biphenyls* (PCB) label and is leaking fluid. The captain takes the following actions:
      I. Contacts the person in charge of the premises in order to determine the amount of hazardous material involved
     II. Orders a firefighter equipped with a handie-talkie to deactivate the transformer and to remain by the switch as a safety precaution
    III. Evacuates the floor area and keeps to a minimum the amount of time that firefighters are exposed to the hazard

    Of the following choices, which one contains only those actions taken by the captain that are CORRECT?
      A. I, II   B. I, III   C. II, III   D. I, II, III

6.___

7. Upon arriving at a fire in an old law tenement, the captain   7.___
   encounters a *white ghost* condition emanating from the oil
   burner room in the cellar.
   In this situation, the captain should order the evacuation
   of the building giving special attention to evacuating the
      A. top floor apartment
      B. apartments adjacent to the light and air shaft
      C. apartment directly over the boiler room
      D. apartments adjacent to the dumbwaiter shaft

8. Upon arriving at the scene of a refrigerant leak in an   8.___
   ice cream factory, the captain of the first arriving unit
   is advised by the building engineer that the system
   contains refrigerants classified as Group I by Chapter 19
   of the Administrative Code.
   In planning his course of action, the captain should treat
   these refrigerants as those which, under normal conditions,
   are
      A. nontoxic, nonflammable, and nonirritating
      B. somewhat toxic, somewhat flammable, and somewhat
         irritating
      C. very toxic, very flammable, and very irritating
      D. very toxic and very irritating, but nonflammable

9. The officer in command at a fire scene orders an engine   9.___
   company captain to have his unit extinguish a large open
   vat of burning lacquer thinners.
   If each of the foams listed below are available, the
   captain should, in most circumstances, use _____ foam.
      A. AFFF   B. alcohol-type
      C. fluoroprotein   D. Hi-Ex

10. A captain in command of the first arriving unit at a   10.___
    large outside fire is concerned about the effects of
    radiant heat on exposed buildings.
    Which one of the following principles of heat radiation
    should the captain consider in determining the proper
    action to take?
       A. Rough surfaces absorb less radiant heat than smooth
          polished surfaces.
       B. Combustible materials which are poor heat conductors
          ignite more readily from heat radiation than materi-
          als which are good conductors.
       C. A thin film of water applied over window glass stops
          little of the radiant heat energy.
       D. The presence of heat radiation can usually be
          detected by observing the wavy lines it creates in
          the air.

11. The captain of the first arriving ladder company at an   11.___
    incident involving the transportation of hazardous
    materials obtains the shipping papers from the driver
    of the truck.
    The captain should expect to find all of the following
    information on the shipping papers EXCEPT

A. the name or category of the product being carried on
   the truck
B. an indication that hazardous materials are carried
   on the truck
C. a copy of the fire department permit and the permit
   number
D. the four digit UN # assigned by DOT to all regulated
   hazardous chemicals

12. Assume that you are the captain of the second ladder   12.___
    company to arrive at a fire on the first floor of a
    detached peak roof private dwelling with a heavy smoke
    and heat condition.
    Which one of the following actions should you direct your
    outside team to take in order to assist in venting?
    A. Avoid the use of porch or garage roofs as a platform
       for venting the upper floors since there will be no
       protection from fire venting from below.
    B. Vent under overhanging eaves only when the window is
       more than three feet below the eaves.
    C. Ascend a portable ladder for proper window ventila-
       tion since this cannot be accomplished from yard
       level by dropping a ladder against the window.
    D. Keeping the tool on an angle so glass doesn't slide
       down the handle, break the lower pane of the window
       first, and then break the upper pane.

13. A captain of a ladder company operating at the scene of a   13.___
    cellar fire in a taxpayer orders one of his members to cut
    a ventilation hole in the first floor.
    The captain should ensure that this cut is made
    A. at a 45° angle to the floor joists
    B. at right angles to the floor joists
    C. in the main aisle
    D. away from the windows

14. A ladder company captain is faced with the problem of   14.___
    forcing entry into a store at 0200 hours. The building
    is equipped with several manually operated rolldown
    security doors which are closed and locked. A piece of
    red reflective adhesive tape which is one inch wide and
    two feet long has been affixed to one of the doors,
    horizontally, at eye level.
    The captain should conclude that the tape MOST likely
    indicates that
    A. a night watchman is on duty in the store
    B. the door is covering the store entrance
    C. hazardous materials are stored in the building
    D. the door is covering a permanently sealed entrance

15. A ladder company captain is responding to a fire in a   15.___
    school which has physically handicapped non-ambulatory
    students in attendance. He wants to locate windows in
    holding areas which are designated for the removal of
    handicapped students.

These windows have red sills and a sign attached to the outside top window pane which reads
    A. F.D. ACCESS   B. HANDICAPPED STUDENTS
    C. HOLDING AREA   D. NON-AMBULATORY STUDENTS

16. The captain of the first arriving ladder company at a fire on the 35th floor of a 40-story high-rise office building directs his unit to take a *Fireman Service* elevator, which services all floors, to proceed to the fire.
The captain's action is
    A. *appropriate*, mainly because this elevator is under the full control of fire department members
    B. *inappropriate*, mainly because these elevators should be operated only by the building management
    C. *appropriate*, mainly because these elevators should be used for fires above the 6th floor
    D. *inappropriate*, mainly because these elevators are capable of being affected by fire on any floor

17. The captain of the first unit to arrive at the scene encounters a fire in a 5-story factory building which was constructed in compliance with the State Labor Law in 1929 and contains a medium hazard occupancy on the fourth floor.
In order to implement the initial attack on the fire, he should be aware that the building
    A. may be non-fireproof because it is five stories high
    B. is required to be fireproof because it is five stories high
    C. may be non-fireproof because of the medium hazard occupancy
    D. is required to be fireproof because of the medium hazard occupancy

18. A covering captain in command of a fireboat responds to the scene of a collision between a freighter and a tanker. Reports indicate that there is a small fire in hold number 1 of the freighter and oil is leaking from tank number 2 of the tanker.
From the information given, the captain should conclude that the
    A. fire is near the bow of the freighter and the leak is near the bow of the tanker
    B. leak is near the stern of the tanker and the fire is near the bow of the freighter
    C. fire is near the bow of the freighter and further information is needed to determine the location of the leak
    D. leak is near the bow of the tanker and further information is needed to determine the location of the fire

19. The captain of the first due engine company arrives at a   19.___
    fire on the first floor of a 4-story non-fireproof factory
    built in 1915 in which artificial flowers are manufactured
    on the first and second floors and candles are manufactured
    on the third and fourth floors. Since a chief has not yet
    arrived at the scene, the captain orders the chauffeur to
    find the sprinkler siamese and to hook up to it in order
    to get water on the first floor fire.
    The captain's action is
    A. *appropriate*, mainly because the building should be
       sprinklered on all four floors
    B. *inappropriate*, mainly because there may not be a
       sprinkler system since the occupancies are medium
       hazards
    C. *inappropriate*, mainly because there may not be a
       sprinkler system since the building is only four
       stories high
    D. *inappropriate*, mainly because the building is
       required to have a sprinkler system only on the third
       and fourth floors

20. A captain arriving at an emergency scene finds a person   20.___
    in need of rescue breathing. He also ascertains that the
    victim is a neck-breather.
    It would be MOST appropriate for the captain to instruct
    the firefighter administering the rescue breathing to
    A. ensure that the victim's head is tilted while deliver-
       ing rescue breathing through the neck opening
    B. assume the victim has no connection between the
       mouth and windpipe and that sealing the nose and
       mouth is necessary
    C. place one hand over the neck opening and administer
       rescue breathing through the mouth or the mouth and
       nose
    D. give ventilation directly through the tracheotomy
       tube if one exists

21. A captain arriving at the scene of a motor vehicle acci-   21.___
    dent encounters a victim bleeding severely from above
    his wrist which is obviously broken.
    It would be MOST appropriate for the captain to order
    members to control the bleeding INITIALLY by
    A. using the brachial artery as a pressure point
    B. elevating the arm above heart level
    C. applying a tourniquet above the wrist area
    D. using the femoral artery as a pressure point in
       conjunction with direct pressure on the wound

22. During overhauling operations at a fire in an H-type   22.___
    multiple dwelling, a captain notices that the cornice is
    hanging loosely.
    Which one of the following safety precautions would be the
    MOST appropriate for the captain to order members to take
    in securing the cornice?

A. Use a ladder roller between the rope and a rough surface if the rope is subject to friction against an abrasive substance.
B. Perform the operation from an area below and on the windward side of the loose cornice.
C. Don a safety harness and secure themselves by a utility rope if working near the edge of the roof.
D. Perform the operation from an area below and on the leeward side of the loose cornice.

23. While conducting a drill on overhauling operations, a captain reminds his firefighters that they should exercise caution during the overhauling of large taxpayer ceilings. The captain would be CORRECT if he specifically tells the firefighters that   23.___
    A. only one suspended ceiling will be found in these buildings because the existing ceiling must be removed prior to installing a new one
    B. ceilings suspended by lightweight wood strips are quickly affected by fire while those suspended by steel wire or bars are not
    C. lightweight lay-in ceiling panels are particularly hazardous since they tend to fall in large sections and cause severe injuries
    D. suspended ceilings constructed of heavy wire lath and plaster or tin can often fail and fall in one piece over the entire area of the store

24. A captain is supervising his unit in overhauling operations in a commercial building which was constructed using tensioned concrete. The roofman informs the captain that he is going to use the power saw with the silicon carbide blade to cut through the concrete and the exposed stranded cables used for tensioning the concrete.   24.___
    Of the following, it would be MOST appropriate for the captain to tell the roofman that this procedure is
    A. *proper*
    B. *improper*, mainly because the stranded cables must not be cut
    C. *improper*, mainly because the bolt cutters should be used
    D. *improper*, mainly because the power saw is not capable of cutting through the concrete

25. A captain is in command of the first arriving engine company at a cellar fire in a row frame building.   25.___
    The captain would be CORRECT to order the first hose line stretched
    A. via the outside front cellar entrance
    B. through the front door then to the cellar via the interior stairs
    C. via the outside rear cellar entrance
    D. through the front door to the parlor floor

26. A captain in command of the second due engine company   26.___
    arrives simultaneously with the first due engine at an
    upper floor fire in a 30-story office building.
    Which one of the following actions should the captain of
    the second due engine order his unit to perform FIRST?
       A. Assist the first due engine in stretching the first
          line from the standpipe.
       B. Stretch a back-up line to the fire floor to protect
          the first line.
       C. Stretch a line to the floor above the fire to protect
          the search team.
       D. Provide handie-talkie communications at the stand-
          pipe outlet until operations begin.

27. The captain of an engine company is operating at the   27.___
    scene of a fire where Hi-Ex foam had been used to flood
    the cellar. The captain is ordered into the foam-filled
    area to operate a hose line to complete extinguishment
    of the fire.
    In this situation, it would be MOST appropriate for the
    captain to order members to
       A. enter the area slowly using a wide fog stream,
          sweeping the floor to wash away any remaining hot
          embers
       B. use the hose line as a substitute for a life line
          when entering the foam-filled area
       C. use the narrow fog stream position and sweep the
          ceiling to cool the area by channeling the heat and
          gases away
       D. wash the foam down to waist level to provide both a
          safe path through the foam and a maximum protective
          shield

28. A captain is examining a fire scene for indications of   28.___
    arson.
    Which one of the following conclusions, if drawn by the
    captain, would be CORRECT?
       A. The point of origin is always an exact point.
       B. Deepest char is sometimes found at the point of
          origin.
       C. Fire dropping down through tongue and groove flooring
          is always an indication of arson.
       D. Small crazing of glass sometimes indicates that
          windows were in place at the start of operations.

29. A captain of a ladder company arrives at the scene of a   29.___
    small garage fire that has been extinguished by the first
    due engine company. The lieutenant of the engine company
    tells the captain that he feels the fire is suspicious
    and that an odor of rotten cabbage had been detected in
    the garage.
    This odor should lead the captain to suspect that the
    substance that may have been used to ignite the fire was
       A. hydrogen cyanide   B. phosphorous
       C. phosgene   D. carbon disulfide

30. A captain responds to the scene of an automobile fire.   30.___
Of the following, each is an indication that the fire
may have been intentionally set EXCEPT the
    A. remains of an oil can are found in the engine compart-
       ment
    B. radiator is loose and held in place by hose clamps
    C. gasoline line hoses are broken and have jagged edges
    D. gasoline tank drain plug is found under the car and
       the threaded collar is intact on the tank

31. While inspecting an industrial occupancy, a captain   31.___
observes a pintle on the deflectors of several sprinkler
heads.
The captain should conclude that all these sprinkler
heads are designed with orifices that are _____ $\frac{1}{2}$ inch.
    A. smaller than
    B. exactly
    C. larger than
    D. either smaller or larger than

32. The captain of a ladder company arrives at the scene of   32.___
a fire in an old law tenement that has been converted to
a premises consisting of single room occupancies.
Assuming that the building conforms to all legal requirements, one consideration which the captain should use as
a guideline in determining the proper course of action is
that the building
    A. is required to have sprinklers in each room supplied
       by a roof tank or a fire department siamese connec-
       tion
    B. must be arranged so that each occupant has direct
       access to either the stairs or the fire escape as
       a means of egress
    C. may have rooms with padlocked doors which members
       should bypass during performance of the primary
       search
    D. is required to have an interior alarm system to warn
       occupants of fire

33. The captain of a ladder company is operating on the third   33.___
floor of a 6-story renovated building when he discovers
that the fire has entered a utility shaft.
It would be MOST appropriate for the captain to contact
the roof man via handie-talkie and order him to
    A. remove the metal roof cap from the ventilating duct
       in order to vent the inside of the shaft
    B. immediately proceed to the top floor and open the
       ceiling to provide ventilation for the cockloft
    C. cut a hole next to the soil pipe vent at the top of
       the shaft to make an examination
    D. proceed to the fourth floor via the fire escape to
       check for fire extension via the shaft

34. A roofman operating at an elevator shaft fire notices an 34.___
opening covered by steel grating in the floor of the
machinery room at the top of the shaft. The roofman asks
the captain, via handie-talkie, the reason for this
opening.
The captain should reply that the opening
   A. provides for air movement in the shaft when the
      elevator goes up and down
   B. is an access point to the emergency shut-off panel
   C. is designed for emergency evacuation when the
      elevator is stuck in the upper part of the shaft
   D. is used to locate the elevator in the shaft when
      there is a serious fire in the elevator pit

35. During operations at a heavy top floor fire in a Class A, 35.___
H-type, non-fireproof multiple dwelling built in 1930,
a ladder company captain receives a handie-talkie trans-
mission from his roofman informing him that *the building
has transverse stairs throughout*.
This information is important because transverse stairs
in this type of operation are a(n)
   A. *disadvantage*, since they limit access between stairs
      in adjoining wings and curtail line stretching options
   B. *advantage*, since they allow access between adjoining
      wings via the public hall and maximize line stretch-
      ing options
   C. *disadvantage*, since they have limited floor landing
      areas and do not provide access between stairs
   D. *advantage*, since they provide access between wings
      and are usually located adjacent to each other

36. The captain of a ladder company reporting to the lobby 36.___
command post at a high-rise fire is directed to report
to the staging area on the 21st floor.
It would be MOST appropriate for the captain to ensure
that his members bring with them a mask and
   A. a spare cylinder for each member, a set of forcible
      entry tools, a search rope, and a utility rope
   B. a spare cylinder for each member except for the
      chauffeur, a set of forcible entry tools, a search
      rope, and a utility rope
   C. a spare cylinder for each member, two sets of
      forcible entry tools, and six foot hooks, a search
      rope, and a utility rope
   D. two sets of forcible entry tools, and a spare
      cylinder for each member except the chauffeur, six
      foot hooks, a search rope, and a utility rope

37. The captain of the first arriving ladder company at a 37.___
fire on the third floor of an E-type multiple dwelling
is informed by the dispatcher that the second ladder
company will be delayed. The captain then orders a
member to the apartment above the fire. The member
inspects the apartment and informs the captain that he
has discovered several hot spots in the walls.

In this situation, the captain should IMMEDIATELY
- A. proceed to the top floor and check for extension of fire into the cockloft
- B. order the member to proceed to the top floor and check for extension of fire into the cockloft
- C. order the member to make small holes in the walls and make a visual check of the bays
- D. order the member to pull the ceiling on the fire floor directly below the hot spots

38. The captain of a ladder company considers taking the following safety precautions at the scene of an electrical power emergency where power lines are down in the street:
- I. Establish a safety zone whose span is equal to the affected span in order to eliminate the possibility of exposure to the voltage gradient.
- II. Instruct members to avoid contact with guy-wires since damaged knuckles can allow the guy-wires to become charged.
- III. Ensure that all members of his unit are wearing their rubber boots which will protect them from the energized wire.

Which one of the following choices contains only those safety precautions where the protection afforded the members is PROPERLY described?
A. I *only*   B. II *only*   C. III *only*   D. I, II, III

38.___

39. Company commanders are responsible for arranging and maintaining the schedule for the control of inspectional activities in all occupancies classified as motion picture theatres.
These inspections should be scheduled
- A. quarterly, approximately one half hour prior to opening
- B. monthly, approximately one half hour prior to opening
- C. quarterly, when the theatre is open to the public
- D. monthly, when the theatre is open to the public

39.___

40. The captain of an engine company has issued a summons and confiscated a kerosene space heater.
The captain is required to forward copies of all the following documents to the Counsel to Department, Legal Affairs, EXCEPT for the
- A. court case records
- B. receipt issued to the person in charge of the premises where the heater was confiscated
- C. invoice/receipt with all particulars
- D. summons

40.___

KEY (CORRECT ANSWERS)

1. D	11. C	21. A	31. C
2. D	12. C	22. A	32. D
3. A	13. B	23. D	33. C
4. A	14. B	24. B	34. A
5. D	15. A	25. B	35. B
6. B	16. D	26. A	36. C
7. C	17. B	27. C	37. C
8. A	18. C	28. B	38. B
9. B	19. A	29. D	39. D
10. B	20. D	30. C	40. D

TEST 2

DIRECTIONS: Each question or incomplete statement is followed by several suggested answers or completions. Select the one that BEST answers the question or completes the statement. *PRINT THE LETTER OF THE CORRECT ANSWER IN THE SPACE AT THE RIGHT.*

1. As a company commander, you determine that there is a need   1.___
   for fire prevention education among the residents of your
   unit's administrative district. Accordingly, you decide
   that all private dwellings where access is permitted should
   be inspected.
   In order to do this, you must obtain final approval from
   the
   A. battalion fire prevention coordinator
   B. division fire prevention coordinator
   C. borough commander
   D. fire commissioner

2. A captain is conducting a drill in which he is discussing   2.___
   various aspects of altered buildings in his administrative
   district. He makes the following statements:
     I. Pertinent fire prevention records should be reviewed
        on a monthly basis
    II. The approval of the borough commander must be secured
        before a pre-fire plan will be required
   III. The captain should have an index maintained indicating
        whether the alteration is major or minor and the name
        of the officer or inspector making subsequent inspec-
        tions

   Which one of the following choices includes only those
   statements that are CORRECT?
   A. I, II   B. I, III   C. II, III   D. I, II, III

3. An engine company captain is inspecting a construction   3.___
   site within his administrative district at which explosives
   are being used and stored.
   Which one of the following conditions observed by the
   captain constitutes a violation?
   A
   A. third class magazine contains 210 pounds of explosives
   B. magazine containing blasting caps is located 90 feet
      from a magazine containing explosives
   C. blaster is capping a cartridge 55 feet from a fifth
      class magazine containing explosives
   D. magazine contains black powder stored in 25 lb.
      metallic cans

4. A captain is supervising the inspection of an explosives   4.___
    magazine which is located in his district. A permit has
    been issued for the demolition of a structure by use of
    explosives.
    The captain should be aware that, unless a special permit
    has been granted by the fire commissioner, above ground
    blasting on the site is limited to daylight hours, from
    Monday through _____, between _____ P.M.
        A. Friday; 7 A.M. and 7   B. Friday; 8 A.M. and 6
        C. Saturday; 7 A.M. and 7   D. Saturday; 8 A.M. and 6

5. A captain on hydrant inspection duty in his administrative   5.___
    district comes upon hydrants painted yellow on an express-
    way.
    Of the following choices, which one should the captain use
    as a guideline in dealing with these hydrants?
        A. All assigned first alarm engine and ladder companies
           have been issued a curb valve key for these hydrants.
        B. The captain must maintain a second curb key, painted
           yellow, locked in the company office.
        C. The curb valves of these hydrants are open from
           October 15 through May 15.
        D. The curb valve should be fully opened before opening
           the hydrant.

6. A captain conducting semi-annual hydrant inspection   6.___
    notices a red hydrant with the letters HPFS printed on
    the barrel.
    The captain should recognize this hydrant as a
        A. high pressure hydrant on a low pressure main
        B. low pressure hydrant on a high pressure main
        C. high pressure hydrant to be reserved for maxi-water
           unit use
        D. low pressure hydrant to be reserved for maxi-water
           unit use

7. A captain is in charge of a unit which has returned to   7.___
    quarters after operations which required the use of masks.
    The captain then supervises the inspection of all masks
    carried by the unit.
    Of the following actions, which one should the captain
    take concerning the results of this inspection?
        A. Replace out-of-service masks with spares from the
           battalion pool.
        B. Record the results of this inspection on the mask
           record card for each mask inspected.
        C. Forward any defective masks along with requisitions
           for necessary repairs to the Division of Training.
        D. List any defects found and the results of the inspec-
           tion in the office record journal.

8. An engine company captain notices an odor of gasoline in   8.___
the cellar of company quarters shortly after a gasoline
delivery.
After shutting down any ignition sources, ventilating the
area, and taking the necessary safety precautions, it
would be MOST appropriate for the captain to
  A. notify the Fuel Desk, Bureau of Operations and forward
     the necessary requisitions
  B. notify the Department of Buildings and forward a
     special report to the Hazardous Materials Unit
  C. notify the fire department buildings unit and forward
     the necessary requisition
  D. notify the fuel oil company that made the delivery
     and forward a special report to the fire commissioner

9. Captains are mandated by department rules and regulations   9.___
to have firefighters in their respective units check,
operate, and inspect certain firefighting equipment every
Monday during the 9x6 tour.
Which one of the following choices lists the equipment
that must be operated or inspected during this tour?
  A. Life belts, emergency electrical power generator, bulk
     foam storage tank, seat belt
  B. Lifesaving rope, Hurst tool, handie-talkie, reserve
     apparatus
  C. Life belts, masks, portable electrical generator,
     hand holds, and rails
  D. Lifesaving rope, resuscitators, survey meters, spare
     apparatus

10. A captain who is conducting a semi-annual safety equipment   10.___
inspection condemns a firefighter's helmet. The firefighter appeals that decision to the borough commander,
who finds that the helmet is repairable. The helmet is
then sent to the manufacturer for repair.
Then, after receiving the repaired helmet from the manufacturer, the helmet along with the manufacturer's invoice
must be submitted for approval to the
  A. chief of department   B. borough commander
  C. division commander   D. battalion commander

11. An on-duty firefighter in your unit tells you that she   11.___
has been discriminated against in regard to her transfer
application.
You should advise her that at this point she may
  A. request an informal adjustment of the complaint with
     the borough commander
  B. be given reasonable time during the current tour to
     discuss the matter with the Transfer Desk, Bureau of
     Personnel
  C. report to the Equal Employment Opportunity Unit in
     person during the current tour to register the
     complaint
  D. contact the Equal Employment Opportunity counselor
     designated to cover her unit

12. Which one of the following statements made by a captain to 12.____
one of his lieutenants about the situational stress and
substance abuse policy in the fire department is CORRECT?
   A. Unit officers are urged to refer members who show
      signs of mental illness to the Counseling Service
      Unit.
   B. If a member who is diagnosed as being mentally ill
      refuses to cooperate with recommended treatment, a
      referral will be made to the office of the inspector
      general.
   C. If a member who is a substance abuser refuses to
      comply with recommended treatment, a referral will be
      made to the office of the inspector general.
   D. If a member who refuses treatment for substance
      abuse is found unfit for duty, he shall be suspended
      by the Chief Medical Officer.

13. A unit commander is implementing command discipline for a 13.____
member who has failed to observe safety precautions while
responding to an alarm.
Of the following penalties, the unit commander would be
acting PROPERLY if he imposes
   A. suspension of early relief privileges for a maximum
      of 4 months
   B. suspension of mutual exchange of tours privileges
      for a maximum of 4 months
   C. a detail of the member away from the unit for a
      maximum of 4 months
   D. the forfeiture of a maximum of 6 vacation days

14. A captain has preferred charges against a member and a 14.____
pre-trial conference is scheduled to be held subsequent
to the service of charges. The presiding officer of the
conference will render a written recommendation within
ten days.
Assuming that the fire commissioner approves the recommendation and the respondent waives the right to a trial,
the recommendation shall be dispositive of the issue if
   A. the respondent accepts the recommendation
   B. both the respondent and complainant accept the
      recommendation
   C. the respondent, complainant, and inspector general
      accept the recommendation
   D. both the respondent and inspector general accept the
      recommendation

15. A company commander working a 9x6 tour who is notified 15.____
that one of his members has been suspended from duty must
take certain actions relating to the member's official
badges, insignia, and other department property.
Which one of the following would be a CORRECT action for
the captain to take in such a situation?

A. Order the member to turn these items over to Bureau of Personnel within 48 hours.
B. Collect and forward these items to the inspector general immediately.
C. Order the member to return these items to the Badge Desk until the suspension is revoked.
D. Collect and retain these items until the suspension is revoked.

16. You are preparing a drill on firefighting operations at Transit Authority facilities.
Which one of the following points should you include in the drill?   16.___
    A. At subway operations, evacuating passengers will always be given priority use of emergency exits even if these exits are the most direct means of access to the fire area.
    B. When an engine company is connecting the pumper to the hydrant, the chauffeur should always select the hydrant closest to the subway entrance to reduce the amount of hose in the stretch.
    C. At any subway fire, two engine companies must be used to stretch the initial hose line.
    D. Small fires in the ties of an elevated railroad should be extinguished by a handline in a tower ladder basket whenever possible.

17. Which one of the following points should be stressed by a captain who is preparing a company drill concerning compactor fires?   17.___
    A. The shut-off for the compactor must be located on the wall just outside the compactor room.
    B. The outside vent man should provide ventilation of the compactor room from the exterior.
    C. The ladder company chauffeur should assist in the search and venting procedures or provide special tools.
    D. Compactor rooms must have a garden hose for use in wetting down debris from the chute.

18. A captain is preparing a drill on the variance granted the oil heating industry to transport limited amounts of combustible liquids as specified in the fire prevention information bulletin.
Of the following statements, which one should NOT be included in the drill?
The fuel   18.___
    A. must be carried in a service van, rather than in a private vehicle
    B. is to be dispensed into a fill line only
    C. is limited to #2 fuel oil only
    D. must be carried in safety cans having the maximum capacity of five gallons

19. A captain is conducting a critique concerning a recently   19.___
    concluded fire operation.
    It is MOST advisable for the captain to begin the
    critique by
        A. asking members if they experienced any difficulties
           in accomplishing their individual assignments
        B. identifying the most serious aspects of the operation
        C. discussing the problems that lend themselves to
           immediate solutions
        D. focusing on the positive aspects of the operation

20. Upon returning to quarters from a fire in a high-rise   20.___
    office building where elevator problems were encountered,
    the captain decides to conduct a critique on methods of
    recalling elevators.
    Which one of the following points should the captain
    discuss during the critique?
        A. Elevators can be automatically recalled by a water
           flow from a sprinkler system.
        B. By placing the keyed switch in the lobby in the
           Fireman Service position, only the *Fireman Service*
           elevators in that bank will return to the street
           lobby.
        C. The *Emergency Stop* buttons will be the only controls
           remaining operable in the elevator during recall.
        D. When the elevator car reaches the street lobby and
           the car doors open, return the keyed switch in the
           lobby to the *normal* position.

21. A captain is conducting a critique of a fire which   21.___
    occurred in a 6-story fireproof department store which
    was constructed in 1986. The building is 80 feet wide x
    80 feet high x 90 feet deep and all floors have public
    access and are served by elevators, unenclosed escalators,
    and enclosed stairways. During the critique, one of the
    firefighters asks the captain if this building is required
    by the Building Code to have a sprinkler system.
    The captain should answer that a sprinkler system is
        A. *not required*
        B. *required*, mainly because of the height and area of
           the building
        C. *required*, mainly because of the unenclosed escalator
        D. *required*, mainly because the public is permitted above
           the street floor

22. During semi-annual inspection of safety equipment, the   22.___
    company commander orders a firefighter to repaint his
    helmet.
    Of the following, the captain should instruct the fire-
    fighter to
        A. clean the helmet with neatsfoot oil to remove as much
           surface dirt as possible before repainting
        B. lightly sand the entire helmet with coarse sandpaper
           so that the roughened surface will allow the paint
           to stick

C. avoid sanding the stitch lines of the helmet and use a mild paint remover in this area to prevent damaging of the threads

D. apply several light coats of high quality oil gloss enamel of the appropriate color

23. The company commander assigns one lieutenant to compile a list of unsafe acts which is to be used for training members at a company drill. The following three statements are included in the list:

   I. Member wears earrings when responding to fires and emergencies

  II. Member operating on roof positions himself so that hose line is between the member and the roof edge

III. Member positions himself between the apparatus and the edge of the pier while the pumper is drafting water.

Of the following choices, which one lists ONLY those statements which should be included on the lieutenant's list of unsafe acts?

   A. I *only*   B. II *only*   C. III *only*   D. I, II, III

23.___

24. An engine company captain arriving early for a tour of duty observes his unit returning from a response. Two members are riding the rear step and two are in the crew cab.

The captain should take

   A. no action because members in pairs can use the rear step when returning from alarms

   B. corrective action because the rear step can only be used as a riding position when responding

   C. no action because members can use the rear step at any time when assigned in pairs

   D. corrective action because the rear step is never to be used as a riding position

24.___

25. During a multi-unit drill, a captain is directing his unit in the use of an eductor to dewater a flooded cellar. During this operation, which one of the following actions should the captain instruct members to take?

   A. Place the intake end of the eductor on the bottom of the removal water only near the conclusion of operations.

   B. Make a prominent mark on the eductor at the beginning of operations so that changes in the water level may be noted.

   C. Set the pumper discharge pressure at 150 psi plus 25 lbs. for each 50 feet of $2\frac{1}{2}$ inch hose used to supply the eductor.

   D. Operate without the strainer attached if debris threatens to clog the intake.

25.___

26. A captain preparing unit members for evaluation by the   26.___
Division of Training makes the following statements about
dangerous gases produced by a typical room fire:
   I. Carbon monoxide is produced by incomplete combustion
     of many common materials; when inhaled, it crowds
     oxygen from the blood and affects the brain and other
     tissues
  II. Nitrogen oxide is produced by burning wallpaper and
     lacquered wall coverings; it is tasteless but has a
     musty hall smell
III. Hydrogen chloride is produced by burning plastics,
     rubberized flooring, and pipes made with PVC; HCL is
     colorless, has a pungent odor, and is intensely
     irritating to eyes and respiratory tract.

Which one of the following choices contains only those
statements that are CORRECT?
  A. I, II   B. I, III   C. II, III   D. I, II, III

27. During a major city-wide drill on air support for high-   27.___
rise building fires, a newly assigned ladder company
captain responds to the mobilization point and orders
that the necessary equipment be placed aboard the helicopter for the high rise roof team.
The captain must make certain that all of the following
are placed on board EXCEPT
  A. 2 Halligan tools
  B. 2 axes
  C. 2 lifesaving ropes
  D. 6 SCBA's with 1-hour cylinders

28. At a multi-unit drill, the captain of a ladder company   28.___
orders the roofman to adjust the belt on the portable
partner saw, series 1200, for proper belt tension.
Which one of the following actions should the captain
ensure is taken by the roofman?
Loosen
  A. and retighten the belt tension bolt first and then
    loosen and retighten the guard knob
  B. both the belt tension bolt and guard knob and then
    retighten them
  C. and retighten the guard knob first and then loosen
    and retighten the belt tension bolt
  D. and retighten the belt tension bolt only, then check
    the guard knob for proper positioning

29. While working in Engine Co. 99, which is located in   29.___
Battalion 65, a covering captain who is assigned to
Division 16, which is quartered with Engine Co. 200,
receives a line-of-duty injury that requires a DOSH-400
entry.
The captain should ensure that this entry is made on the
DOSH-400 at
  A. Engine Co. 99   B. Battalion 65
  C. Division 16   D. Engine Co. 200

30. Company commanders must ensure that 5-gallon cans of
    fluoroprotein foam are carried on each engine and ladder
    apparatus.
    The MINIMUM number of 5-gallon cans that should be carried
    is _____ on each ladder and _____ on each engine.

    A. two; two   B. two; three
    C. three; three   D. three; two

    30.___

31. The captain of an engine company equipped with an aluminum
    extension ladder instructs one of his lieutenants to make
    up a control sheet to ensure proper maintenance of the
    ladder.
    Which one of the following procedures should the captain
    make certain the lieutenant includes on the control sheet?

    A. Frayed or twisted manila halyards should be replaced
       with nylon rope.
    B. Light oil should be applied to all contacting
       surfaces to assist in smooth operation of the sections.
    C. Pulleys should be lubricated regularly with a light
       coat of grease to prevent excessive wear on the
       ball-bearings.
    D. Nicks or burrs found during inspection should be
       removed with a fine file to prevent hand injuries.

    31.___

32. A captain receives notice that a firefighter in his unit
    is being promoted. The lieutenant responsible for
    evaluating this member asks the captain if an evaluation
    report is required.
    The captain should answer that an evaluation report on
    the firefighter's performance must be prepared

    A. for the portion of the evaluation year in which
       the firefighter has served in the unit, and the
       original report forwarded to the firefighter's newly
       assigned unit
    B. for the portion of the evaluation year in which the
       firefighter has served in the unit, and the original
       report forwarded to the Division in the usual manner
    C. *only* if the firefighter has served more than six
       months of the evaluation year in the unit, and the
       original report forwarded to the firefighter's newly
       assigned unit
    D. *only* if the firefighter has served more than six
       months of the evaluation year in the unit, and the
       original report forwarded to the Division in the
       usual manner

    32.___

33. The company commander of Engine Co. 99 is reviewing an
    evaluation report for a 4th grade firefighter with one
    of his lieutenants.
    Of the following, it would be APPROPRIATE for the company
    commander to remind the lieutenant that

    A. the evaluation report should be forwarded to the
       Bureau of Personnel in duplicate at the end of the
       3rd, 6th, 9th, and 11th months of service

    33.___

B. the evaluation period commences on the date of assignment to the company and that prior city service time
does not reduce the probation period

C. extended leaves, such as vacation leave, should not
be granted to 4th grade members during the final
months of probation

D. a copy of the evaluation report must be maintained in
the uniform filing system separate from evaluation
reports of tenured members

34. Which one of the following code letters should a captain
use in the flagging column when making an entry in the
company journal listing tools which were lost at an
operation?
A. LP   B. PL   C. PR   D. TL

34.___

35. The captain of a ladder company observes an imminently
hazardous condition in a building in his district and
decides to request that it be entered immediately into
the CIDS program.
Of the following actions, it would be MOST appropriate
for the captain to
A. complete a CIDS card and contact the dispatcher with
the required information for entry into the computer
B. contact the dispatcher immediately with the information for relay to the staff officer on duty
C. complete a CIDS card and relay the information to
the staff officer on duty via the chain of command
D. contact the staff officer on duty directly with the
information for relay to the dispatcher who will
enter it into the computer

35.___

36. A company commander working a 9x6 tour receives a complaint
that an office building in his district has installed
carpeting on the floor of an exit passageway. An
inspection of the carpeting discloses that it is made of
wool.
With respect to this situation, which of the following is
the MOST complete and accurate listing of the forms which
should be completed?
A. Investigation of complaint report *only*
B. Investigation of complaint report and field inspection report
C. Investigation of complaint report, field inspection
report, and violation order
D. Investigation of complaint report, field inspection
report, court case record, and a summons

36.___

37. A newly promoted lieutenant is in command of an engine
company operating at a 10-26 where a 10-18 has been
transmitted and no chief has responded. The lieutenant
asks the captain in command of the ladder company how to
determine who is responsible for forwarding the fire
report.

37.___

The captain should inform the lieutenant that the report
should be forwarded by the
   A. officer who transmitted the 10-84
   B. officer who transmitted the 10-18
   C. highest ranking officer among the units operating at
      the scene
   D. administrative battalion chief

38. Upon entering quarters for a 6x9 tour on Monday, the   38.___
captain is notified by the off-going lieutenant that
the alarm teleprinter has been inoperative since Sunday
morning. The lieutenant says that Starfire operations
was notified Sunday morning and that an entry was made in
the company journal.
In this situation, the captain should
   A. notify the dispatcher, since the problem has existed
      for more than 24 hours
   B. contact the notification desk at the Bureau of
      Operations since the repairs were not made within
      24 hours
   C. call Starfire operations, since they failed to repair
      the teleprinter within 24 hours
   D. contact the computer assisted dispatch operations
      unit, since the problem has existed for more than 24
      hours

39. A captain inspecting quarters after members have performed   39.___
committee work notices material posted on the kitchen
bulletin board that he feels may be controversial.
According to department regulations, the captain should
   A. remove the material and submit it to the fire
      commissioner for approval before placing it back on
      the bulletin board
   B. remove and discard the controversial material
   C. forward a letterhead report and a copy of the material
      to the borough commander for review before removing
      the material from display
   D. leave the material posted and notify the Equal Employ-
      ment Opportunity office immediately

40. As a company commander, you are required to coordinate an   40.___
ongoing chauffeur training program.
Which one of the following statements is CORRECT con-
cerning this program?
You
   A. should use a company trained chauffeur in preference
      to a detailed school trained chauffeur who is less
      familiar with the response area
   B. must control the mutual exchanges of tours to assure
      the staffing of all apparatus with company trained
      chauffeurs
   C. should make an entry in the office record journal
      when you deem a company trained firefighter profi-
      cient in driving and operating the apparatus
   D. must select members who have the most seniority for
      company chauffeur training

KEY (CORRECT ANSWERS)

1. C	11. D	21. C	31. D
2. B	12. B	22. D	32. B
3. B	13. B	23. A	33. C
4. D	14. A	24. D	34. C
5. D	15. D	25. A	35. C
6. B	16. A	26. B	36. B
7. A	17. C	27. C	37. C
8. C	18. B	28. B	38. D
9. B	19. D	29. A	39. A
10. C	20. A	30. B	40. C

EXAMINATION SECTION
TEST 1

DIRECTIONS: Each question or incomplete statement is followed by several suggested answers or completions. Select the one that BEST answers the question or completes the statement. *PRINT THE LETTER OF THE CORRECT ANSWER IN THE SPACE AT THE RIGHT.*

1. In accordance with department regulations, examination of members' copies of the Book of Regulations is to be conducted by company commanders AT LEAST
    A. annually   B. twice a year
    C. three times a year   D. four times a year

1.___

2. According to department regulations, the *Monthly Statistical Report - Field Inspection Activity* should include company field inspection duty of all
    A. types
    B. types except re-inspection duty on violation orders
    C. types except surveillance inspection duty
    D. types except inspectional duty relative to complaints

2.___

3. During field inspection of a building containing an automobile sprinkler system, you note that the shut-off valves are located where they are not readily accessible. The one of the following procedures to follow in this situation, according to department regulations, is to
    A. write an order to the owner or occupant requiring correction of the physical defect
    B. require no action by the owner or occupant but make special note of the valve location in the building record file
    C. bring to the attention of the owner or occupant the potential water damage hazard inherent in this situation
    D. write an order to the owner or occupant for a sign indicating valve location

3.___

4. Where two or more officers of the same rank are assigned for duty in a company, the senior officer in such rank shall, unless otherwise ordered, exercise command and be responsible for all administrative matters affecting the unit. According to the regulations, the lowest ranking superior officer who has the authority to issue the order underlined above is the
    A. Division Commander
    B. Assistant or Deputy Assistant Chief
    C. Chief in Charge, Bureau of Personnel and Administration
    D. Chief of Department

4.___

5. According to department regulations, the authenticity of   5.___
   all badges and fire line cards displayed by persons within
   fire lines shall be checked, to the extent that other
   responsibilities permit, by
      A. police officers
      B. fire marshals
      C. any uniformed member
      D. officer in command of fire operations

6. Regulations require that each of the following are to be   6.___
   inspected or examined daily EXCEPT
      A. doors, guards, and lights at pole hole openings
      B. hot water and heating installations of quarters
      C. apparatus entrance doors
      D. safety belts

7. When a reasonable doubt exists as to interpretation of an   7.___
   order issued from department headquarters, department
   regulations advise that officers may apply for proper
   interpretation to the
      A. Division Commander
      B. Assistant or Deputy Assistant Chief
      C. Chief in Charge, Bureau of Personnel and Administra-
         tion
      D. Chief of Department

8. According to department regulations, notice of demolition   8.___
   operations about to commence is forwarded to companies for
   each of the following purposes EXCEPT
      A. surveillance inspections during demolition period
      B. alteration in routes of response where affected
      C. enforcing fire department rules for demolition fires
      D. corrective maintenance of building records

9. Regulations state that reports requiring attention of   9.___
   other city departments or agencies are to be forwarded
      A. in duplicate
      B. in triplicate
      C. in quadruplicate
      D. with sufficient copies to provide one for each office
         requiring same

10. Department regulations set forth provisions to be followed   10.___
    in disposing of records of buildings which are demolished.
    The one of the following which is NOT in accord with these
    procedures is that
       A. the word *demolished* is written across the face of the
          building record card
       B. the building record folder is removed from the active
          file and placed in the *dead record file*
       C. a transfer card is filed in place of the building
          record card
       D. a memo is placed in the folder stating when demolition
          work was started and completed

11. While inspecting a business building, you discover an oil   11.___
burner installation with the following features:
    (a) installed on the third story, whose floor is 40'
       above the street level,
    (b) oil delivery lines to the burner are one and one-half
       inches iron pipe size, and
    (c) pressure in the oil lines to the burner is 25 lbs.
       per square inch.
The one of the following statements concerning this
installation and the applicable sections of the rules of
the Board of Standards and Appeals that is MOST accurate is
that
    A. feature A is a violation of the rules
    B. feature B is a violation of the rules
    C. feature C is a violation of the rules
    D. the installation complies with the rules

12. According to the Fire Prevention Code, a person who holds   12.___
a permit for the manufacture of inflammable mixtures and
who wishes to manufacture combustible material is
    A. required to obtain another permit
    B. not required to obtain another permit
    C. not required to obtain another permit unless the mix-
       tures include stove polishes or insecticides
    D. not required to obtain another permit unless the mix-
       tures include medicinal and toilet preparations

13. The one of the following statements which is MOST accurate   13.___
and complete is that the Fire Prevention Code permits the
hanging of fresh-cut decorative greens in places of public
assembly only if they do not contain
    A. pitch
    B. pitch and are hung by means of non-combustible mater-
       ial
    C. pitch, are hung by means of non-combustible material,
       and do not remain for a period in excess of twenty-
       four hours
    D. pitch, are hung by means of non-combustible material,
       have been treated with an approved evaporation retard-
       ing product, and do not remain for a period in excess
       of forty-eight hours

14. In any automatic wet-pipe sprinkler system which has   14.___
standard one-half inch sprinkler heads exposed to cold
and subject to freezing, shut-off valves may be provided
and the water supply discontinued
    A. under no circumstances
    B. from November 15 to March 15 when there are five or
       less such exposed heads
    C. from November 1 to April 1 when there are ten or less
       such exposed heads
    D. from November 15 to April 15 when there are fifteen or
       less such exposed heads

15. At an inspection of a building, one floor of which is used   15.___
    for combustible fibre storage, the following facts are
    revealed:
    (a) The safe bearing capacity of the floor, as certified
        by the Department of Buildings, is 250 lbs/sq.ft.;
        the weight of the combustible fibre is 75 lbs/sq.ft.
    (b) The floor is 10,000 sq.ft. in area, of which 6,000 sq.
        ft. is occupied by the fibre bales
    (c) The height from floor to ceiling is 16', and the
        stacked bales stand 10' high.
    In this situation, _____ violation of the Fire Prevention
    Code.
    A. Item (a) is in   B. Item (b) is in
    C. Item (c) is in   D. there is no

16. The Rules of the Board of Standards and Appeals provide   16.___
    that in a coin-operated dry-cleaning establishment spot-
    ting and sponging may be done by
    A. the general public or a qualified operator if water
       only is used
    B. a qualified operator if water only is used
    C. the general public if water only is used or by a
       qualified operator if inflammable liquids are used
    D. neither the general public nor a qualified operator

17. The MAXIMUM length of unlined linen hose which shall be   17.___
    permitted at any standpipe hose outlet valve is
    A. 50'   B. 75'   C. 100'   D. 125'

18. The State labor law requires that fire drills be conducted   18.___
    monthly in factory buildings over two stories in height in
    which more than 25 persons are employed above the ground
    floor. The one of the following statements that is MOST
    complete and accurate is that the law provides for auto-
    matic exemption from this requirement to factory buildings
    which are completely sprinklered
    A. only
    B. by a system having two adequate sources of water
       supply
    C. by a system having two adequate sources of water
       supply and a maximum number of occupants of any one
       floor not more than 50 percent above the capacity of
       the exits required for the same building if un-
       sprinklered
    D. by a system having two adequate sources of water
       supply, a maximum number of occupants of any one
       floor not more than 50 percent above the capacity of
       the exits required for the same building if un-
       sprinklered and an interior fire alarm system

19. Automatic sprinkler systems installed in the public halls   19.___
    of converted multiple dwellings with a required siamese
    are subjected to a hydrostatic pressure test before
    acceptance. The test pressure for such systems is to be
    NOT less than

A. 30 pounds per square inch
B. 30 pounds per square inch in excess of the normal pressure required for such systems when in service
C. 200 pounds per square inch
D. 200 pounds per square inch in excess of the normal pressure required for such systems when in service

20. According to the rules of the Board of Standards and Appeals, when flame-proofed materials are subjected to prescribed tests, they shall meet established standards for each of the following properties EXCEPT
 A. flashing   B. duration of flame
 C. duration of glow   D. temperature of flame

20.___

21. Of the following duties to be performed, an officer would be LEAST justified in delegating to a member, rather than performing personally, the
 A. inspection of committee work
 B. preparation of a report of an investigation of a complaint
 C. follow-up training of a recently transferred member
 D. making out of hydrant inspection cards

21.___

22. Several times during a drill, an officer restates the major points of his lecture using different words. This teaching technique is MOST appropriate when
 A. one of the men in the group is slower than the rest
 B. the average man in the group finds the material difficult
 C. he himself is somewhat unclear about aspects of the subject matter
 D. the amount of material to be covered would not ordinarily fill the available time

22.___

23. For a captain to permit his lieutenants to participate in the decision-making process is generally desirable, when practicable, primarily because
 A. it leads to the elimination of grievances
 B. better solutions may be obtained
 C. individual development requires an ever-expanding view of operations
 D. the captain is forced to *keep on his toes* under the stimulation of interchange of ideas

23.___

24. When using a standardized survey report form during AFID, it generally is NOT advisable to make an inspection of the facilities in the strict sequence of the items on the form PRIMARILY because the
 A. sequence of the items in the form may not correspond to the physical arrangement of the occupancy or structure
 B. members performing inspection duty will be more likely to make errors of omission rather than commission on the forms

24.___

C. occupancy or structure may require a multi-inspector, multi-page form inspectional approach
D. procedure does not permit distribution of tasks among all the members participating in the inspection

25. While giving job instructions on a new tool, a captain is asked by a member why the operation was not performed in a different manner. The method suggested included some actions which could cause injury. The captain answered that the method he was demonstrating was the correct one, that the suggested method was unsafe, and that there was no point in discussing wrong methods. The captain's approach to the question was

    25.___

A. *proper*, mainly because the members will not have the chance to pick up bad habits
B. *improper*, mainly because the captain did not consider the possibility of modifying the suggestion to make it safer
C. *proper*, mainly because speed of learning is most rapid when only one method is followed
D. *improper*, mainly because hazards of incorrect methods can be avoided if they are known

26. A captain is to hold a drill on a new operation which is long and complicated. The one of the following measures that is MOST important in planning for this drill is to

    26.___

A. reserve sufficient time for the drill so that it can be presented completely and unhurriedly
B. schedule daily repetition of the drill until it is mastered by the group
C. obtain the assistance of experienced members in demonstrating the operation and correcting the performance of members of the group
D. break up the operation into small instructional units and cover one unit at a time

27. Of the following, the MAIN reason for a fire officer to stress safety is to

    27.___

A. develop a respect for danger in all members
B. replace ignorance with practical knowledge leading to the elimination of unfounded fears
C. establish a safety-conscious work atmosphere in which the men seek safer operating methods
D. reduce the degree to which experienced members express impatience and contempt for *restrictive* safety practices

28. *People are ingenious at preserving their points of view and maintaining their biases.* This attitude is LEAST likely to apply to matters relating to

    28.___

A. grievances   B. personnel assignment
C. job skills training   D. fire prevention education

29. A fire officer who, when making assignments, takes into   29.___
    consideration the emotional state of a man under severe
    strain is acting
    A. *improperly*, mainly because the other men will resent
       any signs of favoritism
    B. *properly*, mainly because in some situations the
       affected man may not be dependable
    C. *improperly*, mainly because each man is getting the
       same salary and should be expected to exert the same
       effort
    D. *properly*, mainly because the man will be a more high-
       ly motivated employee when his situation returns to
       normal

30. The outcome that is MOST likely to result from setting   30.___
    work standards slightly higher than subordinates can
    achieve with ease is that they will have
    A. clearly defined and perceivable objectives
    B. a desire to avoid potential failure
    C. the opportunity to enjoy gratifying success
    D. an area about which they can safely complain

31. A recently assigned captain is concerned about the fact   31.___
    that he has taken an instantaneous liking to some of his
    men whereas one just seems to antagonize him. Of the
    following, the MOST useful first step he could take with
    respect to this member is to
    A. determine the chances of transferring him out of the
       company
    B. tactfully ascertain from his lieutenants their reac-
       tions to this man and his reputation as a fireman
    C. recognize that this is the well-known *halo* effect and
       make a conscious effort to be fair to this man
    D. explain his feelings to his chief and ask for his
       advice

32. Safety experts generally regard attempting to determine   32.___
    who is to blame when investigating accidents to be a
    A. *good* practice, mainly because a violation of safety
       rules should not go unpunished
    B. *poor* practice, mainly because an attitude of *covering
       up* makes it difficult to uncover the facts
    C. *good* practice, mainly because persons involved in
       accidents through no fault of their own want to be
       exonerated
    D. *poor* practice, mainly because the multitude of factors
       that *cause* accidents generally makes it difficult, if
       not impossible, to fix the blame

33. A company is faced with a troublesome local problem. The   33.___
    company commander calls all his lieutenants to a meeting,
    outlines the problem, and asks them to give spontaneously
    any ideas that occur to them as possible ways of handling
    it. Each idea suggested is written down, and later
    discussed carefully.

The CHIEF advantage of the procedure employed by the company commander is that
    A. time is not wasted on needless talk
    B. ideas are obtained which otherwise might not be developed
    C. there is less tendency for the meeting to stray from the subject under discussion
    D. lieutenants receive training in analysis of problems and evaluation of solutions

34. While taking up lines during freezing weather, a newly-appointed captain sees a veteran fireman freeing hose from ice by turning it back on himself and pulling it loose. Of the following, the BEST procedure for the officer to follow in this situation is to
    A. question the man to find out whether he knows a better and safer way to perform this work
    B. assign the man to other duties and assign another member to pick up the hose
    C. advise the member that if the hose is damaged he will be subject to charges for abusing department property
    D. order the man to get the necessary equipment to do the job properly

    34.___

35. Before conducting a drill on a new tool, a captain prepared a detailed job breakdown and distributed copies to members of the company several days prior to the drill so that they could become familiar with it beforehand. The MAIN error in the captain's procedure was in
    A. distributing the job breakdown without approval of the Division of Training
    B. distributing the job breakdown before, rather than after, conducting the drill
    C. preparing the job breakdown before conducting the drill and ascertaining the points that cause difficulty
    D. using the job breakdown as an instruction sheet for the learners rather than a teaching tool for the instructor

    35.___

36. When unexpected obstacles arise during the course of operations, the officer must find means of overcoming them. Of the following, the MOST important factor in this endeavor is the officer's
    A. attitude   B. advance planning
    C. training   D. knowledge of procedures

    36.___

37. A new procedure is about to be instituted in your division. Before presenting it to your men, you try to think of what objections they may raise and how to deal with these objections. Of the following, the BEST reason for this practice is that the

    37.___

A. men will respect your competence when you can handle their objections on the spot
B. analysis involved will help you to better understand the new procedure
C. objections can be channeled upwards and the procedure revised before it is implemented
D. knowledge you have of your men's ways of thinking and behaving will be increased

38. A new chauffeur develops a tendency to overspeed the engine before upshifting gears. As his superior, the MOST effective measure for you to take would be to
    A. report the member's deficiency to the Division of Safety
    B. request that the man be relieved of his assignment
    C. institute corrective training emphasizing both theory and performance
    D. discuss this condition with the man to get at its cause

38.____

39. A captain institutes a policy of minimizing the amount of information he passes on to his lieutenants since he feels they are overburdened with details. This practice is
    A. *proper*; it is part of the captain's job to act as a buffer for his men
    B. *improper*; the captain is trying to carry too many responsibilities on his own shoulders
    C. *proper*; his leadership strength is increased by the degree to which is lieutenants turn to him for guidance
    D. *improper*; the lieutenants lack information which may be necessary to proper performance of their duties

39.____

40. While on AFID you come across a clothing factory which shows evidence of poor housekeeping practices. For you to imply to the owner that the fire department will conduct frequent inspections of his premises until satisfactory conditions are maintained is
    A. *proper*, mainly because the owner may be persuaded by it to maintain satisfactory conditions
    B. *improper*, mainly because the owner may feel that he is being harassed
    C. *proper*, mainly because any means which result in the elimination of hazardous conditions are permissible
    D. *improper*, mainly because threats which may not be carried out should not be made

40.____

KEY (CORRECT ANSWERS)

1. D	11. D	21. A	31. B
2. A	12. B	22. B	32. B
3. D	13. C	23. B	33. B
4. D	14. C	24. A	34. D
5. B	15. D	25. D	35. D
6. C	16. B	26. D	36. A
7. C	17. D	27. C	37. A
8. B	18. C	28. C	38. C
9. A	19. C	29. B	39. D
10. A	20. D	30. C	40. A

TEST 2

DIRECTIONS: Each question or incomplete statement is followed by several suggested answers or completions. Select the one that BEST answers the question or completes the statement. *PRINT THE LETTER OF THE CORRECT ANSWER IN THE SPACE AT THE RIGHT.*

1. A company is operating two hose streams at a fire. The reducing tips of the controlling nozzles have been removed. According to department regulations, such tips shall be in possession of the
   A. nozzleman on each line
   B. officer in command of the lines
   C. officer in command at one line and nozzleman on the second line
   D. officer in command at one line and member assisting at the second line

   1.___

2. The one of the following fire gases which causes an increase in breathing rate is
   A. carbon monoxide B. carbon dioxide
   C. sulfur dioxide   D. nitrogen dioxide

   2.___

3. Hosing a safe containing valuable records after it has been exposed to intense fire to cool it and gain access to its contents is GENERALLY a
   A. *good* practice, mainly because the lock mechanism will be protected from further heat damage
   B. *poor* practice, mainly because the safe door may be warped by a sudden drop in temperature
   C. *good* practice, mainly because further charring of the records will be prevented
   D. *poor* practice, mainly because there may be flash ignition of the contents when the door is opened

   3.___

4. A line is to be stretched from a fireboat to shore across open water. The one of the following which would be the BEST estimate of the slack required to permit the charged line to rest on the bottom is
   A. one length
   B. one-tenth of the distance from the fireboat to shore
   C. the depth of water alongside the fireboat
   D. twice the depth of water alongside the fireboat

   4.___

5. The use of draft curtains in combination with automatic sprinklers to provide protection for floor openings will generally prove satisfactory for each of the following purposes EXCEPT
   A. causing sprinklers and sprinkler alarms to operate more promptly
   B. reducing the possibility of an excessive number of sprinklers operating
   C. inducing desired cooling action
   D. preventing smoke spread

   5.___

6. When lowering a person from a roof by means of a roof   6.___
rope, generally, the man doing the lowering should place
the hook of the lifebelt against the _____ knee butted
against the parapet wall.
   A. ledge of the roof with his left
   B. back edge of the roof roller with his left
   C. ledge of the roof with his right
   D. back edge of the roof roller with his right

7. Cofferdams, which consist of the space between two water-   7.___
tight bulkheads, 3 to 6 feet apart, and which can be
flooded to form a fire break, are MOST likely to be found
on
   A. 'tween decks cargo vessels
   B. shelter deck freighters
   C. oil tankers
   D. passenger liners

8. The destructiveness of a dust explosion depends PRIMARILY   8.___
upon the
   A. maximum pressures developed by the explosion
   B. duration of excess pressures
   C. rate of pressure rise
   D. degree of confinement of the explosion area

9. The practice of bringing pumpers close to the fire build-   9.___
ing at greater alarms is generally
   A. *good*, mainly because hose loads may be most efficient-
      ly used
   B. *poor*, mainly because they may be damaged in the event
      of wall collapse
   C. *good*, mainly because the officer in charge of the
      fire will be better able to coordinate the activities
      of his lines
   D. *poor*, mainly because they will interfere with rescue
      and firefighting operations of aerial ladders

10. To obtain a reading of 3 R/hr. on the Model 710 Jordan   10.___
Ion Chamber, the needle position MUST be on the _____ half
of the scale with the range switch in the _____ position.
   A. right; X-1   B. left; X-10
   C. right; X-10   D. left; X-100

11. When supplying an eductor through 2½" cotton-jacketed hose, 11.___
the supply lines should be siamesed or 3" hose used when
the number of lengths from pumper to eductor exceeds
   A. 3   B. 4   C. 5   D. 6

12. The one of the following gases which is GENERALLY flam-   12.___
mable is
   A. sulfur dioxide   B. carbon monoxide
   C. carbon dioxide   D. argon

13. Two types of steel hoops are commonly found on older
    wooden gravity tanks - round hoops and flat ones. The
    one of the following statements concerning such hoops
    that is MOST accurate is that hidden corrosion is a
    serious problem with _____ hoops.
    A. the round hoops but not with the flat
    B. the flat hoops but not with the round
    C. both types of
    D. neither type of

13.___

14. During an oil change, the amount of oil required to refill
    the apparatus engine crankcase is substantially less than
    originally required. This indicates that
    A. the engine is not burning oil
    B. gasoline is leaking into the crankcase
    C. the oil filter should be changed
    D. sludge is present in the oil pan

14.___

15. In the American Standards Association scheme for the
    identification of piping systems, the color code of
    bright blue identifies piping contents as _____ materials.
    A. fire protection   B. dangerous
    C. safe   D. protection

15.___

16. The relay relief valve should be set on all pumpers in a
    relay stretch PRIMARILY because
    A. pressure buildup is distributed evenly when the
       nozzle is shut down
    B. intake pressure on the pumper nearest the nozzle will
       remain at or near a constant figure
    C. excessive pressures caused by a heavy vehicle passing
       over the line will be better dissipated
    D. the multipled effect of a relay pumping stretch is
       not concentrated on those pumpers which do not have
       valves set

16.___

17. The console of the gas analysis system installed in the
    Training Tower of the Division of Training is equipped
    so that it will automatically
    A. follow a pre-set pattern for sampling various loca-
       tions in the fire areas
    B. obtain a continuous written record of the gas sample
       under analysis
    C. select any predetermined fire gas and analyze its
       generation during combustion
    D. reduce air intake and protect thermocouples when
       pyrometer readings exceed 2500°F

17.___

18. Of the following, the MINIMUM amperage in an electrical
    circuit that could possibly create a life hazard is _____
    ampere(s).
    A. 1/10   B. 1   C. 5   D. 10

18.___

19. Examining records of the effectiveness of automatic   19.___
    sprinkler systems on fires in various types of occupancies
    generally is MOST useful for
    A. evaluating the need in these types of occupancies for
       auxiliary firefighting facilities
    B. determining which occupancy types install inferior
       systems
    C. judging which functions within an occupancy type are
       most susceptible to fire
    D. estimating the adequacy of the water sources to these
       systems

20. The volume of water to be supplied to an emergency ammonia 20.___
    mixer depends upon the capacity of the refrigeration sys-
    tem. According to department regulations, this volume of
    water is indicated by the
    A. sign affixed to the siamese or inlet to the mixer
    B. size of the pipe from the siamese or inlet to the
       mixer
    C. manufacturer's identification plate required by law
    D. size of the discharge pipes into the sewer lines

21. The one of the following metal aerial ladders which does   21.___
    NOT have a master throttling switch on the pedestal is
    A. American LaFrance 85'   B. American LaFrance 100'
    C. Mack 85'   D. Mack 100'

22. The smoke produced by plastics involved in fire, compared   22.___
    to smoke produced by wood, in comparable situations,
    usually is
    A. at least twice as much
    B. about the same amount
    C. less than half as much
    D. lower if combustion takes place in normal atmosphere
       and higher if combustion takes place in oxygen-
       deficient atmosphere

23. Comparison of the effectiveness as extinguishing agents   23.___
    of equal amounts of dry chemical and carbon dioxide has
    shown that dry chemical is about _____ more effective.
    A. 10%   B. 50%   C. 100%   D. 200%

24. Water is MOST likely to cause frothing when applied on   24.___
    flammable liquids having a flashpoint
    A. below 100°F   B. between 100°F and 160°F
    C. between 160°F and 212°F D. above 212°F

25. Testing safety belts of members periodically by subject-   25.___
    ing them to a test load equal to or somewhat greater than
    that which would be placed upon the belt if it were
    required to stop a member's fall is inadvisable MAINLY
    because
    A. unnecessary wear on the belts will reduce the usable
       life of the equipment
    B. the test may cause hidden damage to the belt, render-
       ing it unsafe

C. the test may cause members to become overconfident concerning the capacity of the belt to support weight
D. the test stress applied may be exceeded in a real emergency

26. The one of the following materials which has the LEAST tendency to spontaneous heating is
    A. baled hides   B. bagged charcoal
    C. bulk fish scrap   D. boxed mineral wool
                  26.___

27. At a roofed-over lumberyard fire, jumbo fog nozzles were found to be LEAST effective for
    A. covering exposures
    B. controlling smoke
    C. obtaining penetration in depth
    D. reducing the heat generated
                  27.___

28. The effect of applying wallpaper to a new interior finish surface on the flame propagation characteristics of that surface is generally considered
    A. minimal   B. moderate
    C. considerable   D. severe
                  28.___

29. Heat- or smoke-activated self-closing, rolling steel shutters were NOT recommended for use in enclosing the top of escalators between basements and street floor PRIMARILY because
    A. access to the basement is delayed until forcible entry is effected
    B. persons may be trapped as they climb to street floor level
    C. difficult basement ventilation becomes more difficult
    D. persons in the opening may be injured by the closing shutters
                  29.___

30. For common exothermic reactions, fire intensity is always controlled by the _____ the combustible.
    A. nature of   B. state of division of
    C. rate of air supply to   D. physical arrangement of
                  30.___

31. The discharge pattern of the Bresnan Distributor is such that the percentage of the volume that is directed downward is MOST NEARLY
    A. 100%   B. 75%   C. 50%   D. 25%
                  31.___

32. Decomposition of cellulose nitrate yields oxides of nitrogen. The PRIMARY hazard of these gases is that they
    A. may cause fatalities to persons who show no immediate ill effects
    B. are extremely irritating to the eyes, nose, throat, and lungs
    C. cause blistering of the skin and respiratory tract
    D. cause eye impairment that may be of a permanent nature
                  32.___

33.

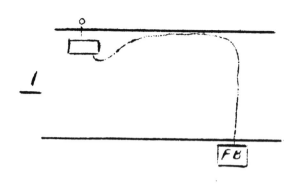

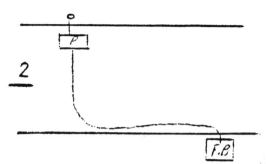

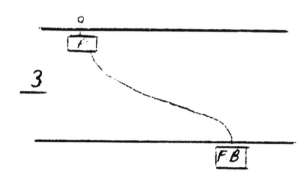

The above sketches show three methods of stretching a hose
line from pumper P to a fire building FB on the other side
of the street. The one of the following statements that
is MOST correct is that only method(s) _____ is(are)
proper.

   A. 1 and 2   B. 1   C. 2   D. 3

34.   The engine pressure required to deliver 300 gallons per
      minute to a 1¼" nozzle through 2500 ft. of siamesed,
      2½" (K = .066) rubber-lined hose is MOST NEARLY _____ psi.
      A. 190   B. 220   C. 250   D. 280

35.   A fire on the 8th floor of a building has caused 20
      sprinkler heads to open. (Assume 12' height per story.)
      An engine pumping through 400' of 2½" rubber-lined hose
      is connected to the siamese of the sprinkler system.
      25 pounds pressure is required at the heads.
      The engine pressure required is MOST NEARLY _____ psi.
      A. 300   B. 325   C. 350   D. 400

36.   Two 1500 ft. lines are siamesed to a single 200 ft. line
      of 2½" rubber-lined hose equipped with a 1¼" nozzle
      (K = .248). One of the parallel lines is 2½" rubber-
      lined hose; the other is 3" rubber-lined hose. Engine A,
      pumping through the 2½" line, is delivering 250 gallons
      per minute. Engine B is then connected to the 3" line.
      The lowest pressure at engine B required to open the
      clapper valve in the siamese to permit water to flow from
      engine B is MOST NEARLY _____ psi.
      A. 65   B. 100   C. 135   D. 170

36

Questions 37-40.

DIRECTIONS: Questions 37 through 40 are to be answered on the
basis of the information given in the following
paragraph.

A mixture of combustible vapor and air will burn only when the
proportion of fuel to air lies within a certain range, i.e., between
the upper and lower limits of flammability. If a third, non-combus-
tible gas is now added to the mixture, the limits will be narrowed.
As increasing amounts of diluent are added, the limits come closer
until, at a certain critical concentration, they will converge. This
is the peak concentration. It is the minimum amount of diluent that
will inhibit the combustion of any fuel-air mixture.

37.   If additional diluent is added beyond the peak concentra-   37.___
tion, the flammable limits of the mixture will
   A. converge rapidly   B. diverge slowly
   C. diverge rapidly   D. not be affected

38.   If the four numbers listed below were peak concentration   38.___
values obtained in a test of four diluents, then the MOST
efficient diluent would have the value of
   A. 7.5   B. 10   C. 12.5   D. 15

39.   The word *inhibit*, as used in the last sentence of the   39.___
above paragraph, means MOST NEARLY
   A. slow the rate of
   B. prevent entirely the occurrence of
   C. reduce the intensity of
   D. retard to an appreciable extent the manifestation of

40.   Of the following graphs shown below, which BEST repre-   40.___
sents the process described in the paragraph?

A.
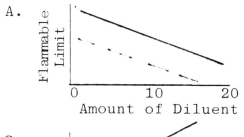

B.
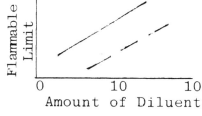

C.
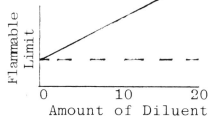

D.
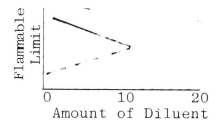

_____ Upper Flammable Limits

---------- Lower Flammable Limits

KEY (CORRECT ANSWERS)

1. B	11. B	21. A	31. B
2. B	12. B	22. A	32. A
3. C	13. B	23. C	33. B
4. D	14. D	24. D	34. A
5. D	15. D	25. B	35. C
6. A	16. C	26. D	36. A
7. C	17. B	27. C	37. D
8. C	18. A	28. A	38. A
9. A	19. A	29. B	39. B
10. C	20. B	30. C	40. D

EXAMINATION SECTION
TEST 1

DIRECTIONS: Each question or incomplete statement is followed by several suggested answers or completions. Select the one that BEST answers the question or completes the statement. *PRINT THE LETTER OF THE CORRECT ANSWER IN THE SPACE AT THE RIGHT.*

1. The *over-and-under* operation type of firefighting approach is generally MOST applicable to _____ fires.   1.___
    A. bulk oil tank   B. lumber yard
    C. aircraft crash   D. structural

2. Where top floor tenement fires have extended to the cock-   2.___
    loft and the roof has been opened up for ventilation, operating streams into these roof openings is generally a
    A. *poor* practice, chiefly because the streams will be directed on smoke rather than on the heart of the fire
    B. *good* practice, chiefly because heated convection currents will be broken up and cooled
    C. *poor* practice, chiefly because heat and smoke may be driven back into the cockloft and top floor
    D. *good* practice, chiefly because a large body of fire can be quickly extinguished

3. In the Halon coding system, each digit represents the   3.___
    number of atoms while the position of the digit in the number represents a specific chemical element.
    For Halon number 1202, the number 1 indicates that the molecule contains one atom of
    A. bromine   B. carbon   C. chlorine   D. fluorine

4. A street vault incident described in a department safety   4.___
    bulletin explains how two persons were asphyxiated when they descended into the vault.
    Tests of the atmosphere of the vault showed that the hazard was due to
    A. light smoke and fumes generated by burning synthetic insulation
    B. gasoline vapors from a leaking underground tank
    C. replacement of oxygen by carbon dioxide
    D. natural gas entering the vault

5. Assume that there is a fire in a machine shop which has   5.___
    a salt bath located in one corner. The salt bath has not yet become involved in the fire.
    The one of the following which is the RECOMMENDED procedure to deal with this situation is to
    A. use a solid stream to cool the bath to lower its temperature below its flash point
    B. use a fog stream to cool the bath below its self-ignition temperature

C. avoid use of water on the bath so as to prevent a
   steam explosion
D. avoid use of water on the bath so as to prevent the
   spreading of a flammable liquid along the floor

6. Of the following, the PRINCIPAL reason for a fireman   6.___
wearing a helmet of the proper size, other than from
the standpoint of comfort, is that
   A. sufficient space will be available for storage of
      small items such as a woolen hat, spare gloves, or
      a small coil of rope
   B. if a helmet fits loosely, its ability to resist
      the transmission of force will be reduced
   C. a tight-fitting helmet will not readily be jarred
      loose by impact
   D. the helmet may be removed faster in case of injury

7. During a drill on the use of oxy-acetylene cutting   7.___
equipment, an officer observes the members practicing
the proper procedure for securing the equipment after
its use.
The one of the following which the members should NOT
do is to
   A. shut down the torch acetylene valve before shutting
      down the torch oxygen valve
   B. shut off both supply tanks in the same order as the
      torch valves were closed
   C. open and close the torch oxygen valve before opening
      and closing the torch acetylene valve to drain the
      lines
   D. secure the regulators by turning the screw valve
      counter-clockwise until loose

8. Of the following, the PRIMARY purpose of holding fire   8.___
tests at a high-rise office building is to
   A. determine the hazard of polyurethane insulation
   B. evaluate the effectiveness of sprinklers with a
      limited water supply
   C. test the effectiveness of stair pressurization
   D. develop procedures for venting the fire floor by
      window vents

9. Recently, a fire occurred in a one-story, non-fireproof   9.___
concrete block wall and metal roof warehouse located
under a bridge.
The one of the following that was NOT one of the three
comparatively recent firefighting innovations that proved
its worth at this fire was
   A. rapid water   B. the superpumper system
   C. partner saws   D. the tower ladder

10. A Protect-A-Guard window gate has been approved for use   10.___
on windows leading to fire escapes.
The PROPER forcible entry method for opening this gate
is to open it from the
  A. *inside* by removing the pin which holds the hasp in
     place
  B. *outside* by prying out the screws that attach the
     hinges to the window frame
  C. *inside* by springing the lock side using the axe and
     Halligan tool
  D. *outside* by striking the latch downward with a sharp
     blow of an axe or Halligan tool

11. The one of the following which is the BEST method of   11.___
extinguishing cellulose nitrate fires is to
  A. shovel sand or graphite around the edges of the
     burning material, gradually covering the whole fire
  B. apply large quantities of water from hose streams
     positioned upwind from the burning material
  C. use CO_2 applied from behind barricades to protect
     against small decomposition explosions
  D. fill the area involved with High-X foam and extin-
     guish any small, deep-seated pockets of fire in the
     material with small water extinguishers or streams

12. Which one of the following was NOT one of the benefits   12.___
gained when the mask service unit took on the responsi-
bility of compressing its own air?
  A. Higher pressure was pumped into the tanks.
  B. Good clean air was supplied to the masks.
  C. A large savings in money resulted.
  D. The department would never run out of a supply of
     air.

13. Liquefied gas types of extinguishing agents as compared   13.___
to vaporizing liquid types generally have _____ reach
and are _____ to disperse.
  A. longer; slower   B. shorter; slower
  C. longer; quicker   D. shorter; quicker

14. When using pressure-sensitive tape in the process of   14.___
removing window glass, the RECOMMENDED procedure is to
start at the
  A. top and strike the glass often to break it into
     small pieces
  B. bottom and strike the glass all over with an axe
     with as much force as possible
  C. top and strike the glass all over with a Halligan
     tool to create a spider-webbing pattern
  D. bottom and strike the glass with sufficient force
     to create openings on all four corners

15. It is beneficial to the operating forces to limit the
    use of fog as a cooling agent in a heated area where
    excessive steam could be produced.
    With respect to department policy, the guidelines pro-
    vided by this statement is generally
    A. *correct*, chiefly because steam can be unbearable and
       CO will concentrate at lower room levels
    B. *incorrect*, chiefly because the smothering effect of
       the steam will result in quickest extinguishment
    C. *correct*, chiefly because the rapid expansion of fog
       into steam reduces its effectiveness as a ventilat-
       ing mechanism
    D. *incorrect*, chiefly because limiting the amount of
       extinguishing agent used is a practice that should
       be avoided when fire damage clearly exceeds poten-
       tial water damage

15.___

16. A *plant* in the language of arson investigation can mean
    each of the following EXCEPT
    A. the material placed about the ignition device to
       feed the initial flame
    B. a fixed surveillance of a limited area
    C. a person who derives a profit from the crime of
       arson
    D. an officer who infiltrates an arson ring

16.___

17. The CDV-700 series geiger counter headphone set is LEAST
    useful for
    A. decontamination operations
    B. use in areas of poor visibility
    C. keeping the eyes free for other tasks
    D. coordinating the count per minute scale with the
       audible signal

17.___

18. Of the following substances, the one that would MOST
    appropriately be protected with a sprinkler installa-
    tion is
    A. cellulose acetate   B. quicklime
    C. magnesium powder   D. calcium carbide

18.___

19. The feeding of firefighters during the lengthy operations
    that may occur when civil disorders break out is a
    problem in logistics.
    The one of the following that is generally considered to
    be an UNDESIRABLE practice is to
    A. contract in advance for box lunches from restaurant
       chains
    B. secure meals from airline caterers
    C. accept voluntary donations of foodstuffs from citizens
    D. request municipal hospitals to supply meals

19.___

20. Bilge sounding pipes generally extend to the upper deck   20.___
    on freighters.
    The openings to these pipes are USUALLY located
       A. near the sides of the ship on each side of each hold
       B. within the deck cowls at the top of ventilator shafts
       C. in vertical shafts extending downward from the mast
          house
       D. under small hatch covers placed over the head of the
          vertical ladders that extend down to the lower hold

―――

KEY (CORRECT ANSWERS)

1.	D	11.	B
2.	C	12.	A
3.	B	13.	D
4.	D	14.	C
5.	C	15.	A
6.	B	16.	C
7.	C	17.	D
8.	C	18.	A
9.	A	19.	C
10.	B	20.	A

―――

TEST 2

DIRECTIONS: Each question or incomplete statement is followed by several suggested answers or completions. Select the one that BEST answers the question or completes the statement. *PRINT THE LETTER OF THE CORRECT ANSWER IN THE SPACE AT THE RIGHT.*

1. Four types of evidence are involved in arson investiga-
   tions.
   The two types of evidence which are generally of GREATEST
   concern to the firefighter are called
   A. documentary and physical
   B. documentary and direct
   C. direct and indirect
   D. direct and physical

   1.___

2. Inhalation of smelling salts is NOT generally recommended
   as a first aid treatment for a victim who has been exposed
   to the fumes of
   A. freon   B. chlorine
   C. sulfur dioxide   D. hydrogen sulfide

   2.___

3. The practice of having police ride fire apparatus during
   periods of civil disorders is considered
   A. *desirable*, chiefly because they will be the objects
      of hostility permitting firemen to fight fire
   B. *undesirable*, chiefly because hostility toward police
      will be transferred to include firefighters
   C. *desirable*, chiefly because hostility towards fire-
      fighters is a common occurrence during civil dis-
      orders
   D. *undesirable*, chiefly because the police presences
      does not reduce the hazard to firemen

   3.___

4. The one of the following which is NOT a reason given by
   Kimball for the practice of calling one or two additional
   companies to a working fire after the first-due companies
   have been working a half hour or more is that it
   A. reduces the chance of sickness due to exposure
   B. reduces the chance of injury due to exhaustion
   C. gives more members experience operating at working
      fires
   D. avoids the appearance of a fire *getting away* to a
      second alarm

   4.___

5. *Light* water would be MOST suitable for use as an extinguishing agent on a fire involving
   A. fuel oil   B. electronic data computers
   C. baled rags   D. raw sugar

   5.___

6. Which one of the following is NOT a recommended method of operating electrically operated security doors on the front of a mercantile building?   6.___
   A. Activate the key switches which are usually found on either side of the door
   B. Remove the housing and raise by means of the chain hoist assembly
   C. Cut the padlock with a bolt cutter and force the door open by the handles at the lower edge
   D. Remove the housing and disconnect the roller chain from the sprocket wheel

7. In addition to its greater load-bearing capacity, the MAIN reason nylon rope was chosen in preference to other ropes in a pilot program studying the Sav-Tee Harness was the finding that nylon rope   7.___
   A. can be manufactured in an *endless* form
   B. has greater abrasion resistance
   C. is less stiff
   D. offers greater impact strength

8. The one of the following cellar pipes which is provided with an *automatic* protective water spray designed to minimize the heat and smoke hazard to the operator manipulating the device from a position above the fire is the   8.___
   A. Hart   B. Baker   C. Rockwood   D. Bent

9. An engine company officer finds that a LNG tank truck has spilled its contents and the LNG has formed a pool. Upon applying water on the pool, the white solid substance floats on the water's surface.
Of the following, the MOST appropriate action for the officer to take upon observing this condition is to   9.___
   A. withdraw his forces from the area and evacuate civilians within a 300-foot radius
   B. allow the white substance to evaporate or burn out under cover of water spray
   C. break up the white substance with heavy solid streams to hasten evaporation and dispersion of the LNG
   D. discontinue application of water on the white substance and cover the surface with foam

10. *Snubbing* on an object is a technique which   10.___
   A. permits a load on a line to be held in place
   B. reduces the likelihood of water damage to the object
   C. makes use of the apparatus to remove obstructions
   D. requires the use of a pallet and a fork-lift truck

11. At a fire in a one-story supermarket, snow on the roof of the building is beginning to melt in a certain area. Of the following, the MOST appropriate action that an officer should take upon receiving this information is to order   11.___

A. withdrawal of all forces from the interior of the structure
B. opening of the roof in the area where the snow is melting
C. washing the snow on the roof towards the area where the snow is melting
D. pulling the ceiling under the area where the snow is melting

12. The one of the following portable extinguishers which operates at the HIGHEST pressure and has the SHORTEST range is
    A. dry chemical   B. soda-acid
    C. carbon dioxide   D. foam

12.___

13. During an inspection of a plant which manufactures paper products, the officer observes completed work being placed in paper cartons. The cartons are then stacked on wooden skids in a separate storage area awaiting shipment.
The one of the following which is generally the MOST appropriate evaluation of the practice described in this situation is that skids
    A. are highly combustible, adding much fuel to the fire
    B. permit excess air flow to fires
    C. minimize water damage losses by raising stock off the floor
    D. provide space under the stock, thus permitting fire to be more readily extinguished

13.___

14. Of the following, the BEST method of overhauling after a large fire involving polystyrene foam products is to
    A. remove the foamed products from the building
    B. soak the foamed material with *wet* water
    C. clear an area on the floor and separate the burned foamed products into a pile while playing a small diameter hose stream on it
    D. dip the burned foamed products in vats or salvage covers filled with water

14.___

15. The application of cold or iced water to burned skin areas is a first aid practice that is generally recommended *provided* that it is
    A. delayed for several minutes and the water is then poured onto the affected areas heavily
    B. done immediately and the water is poured onto the affected areas heavily
    C. delayed for several minutes and the water is then poured slowly over the affected areas
    D. done immediately and the water is poured slowly over the affected areas

15.___

16. Assume that you are in command of a company at a fire
    in a ship's hold. The officer in command of the fire
    orders you to use a Heffernan distributor.
    The distributor SHOULD be supplied by a _____ line at
    _____ psi pump pressure.
        A. 2½"; 200   B. 3"; 150   C. 3½:; 200   D. 3½"; 150

16.___

17. Studies on the fuel-ignition suppression capability of
    foam-covered runways for aircraft conducted by the
    United States Naval Research Laboratory showed that
    foam layers serve as an excellent method of suppressing
    metal-to-runway surface-friction spark ignition of
    aircraft fuels.
    Of the following statements regarding covering runways
    with foam, the LEAST appropriate is that
        A. the critical threshold of foam thickness on the
           runway surface is uncertain
        B. foam facilitates the sliding of an airframe coming
           into contact with it
        C. foam layers are more effective when aged 10 to 15
           minutes
        D. water, settling on the runway surface from the foam
           layer, is the primary agent cooling the metal sparks

17.___

18. The use of water sprays for controlling the path of
    travel of liquefied natural gas vapors or solid hose
    streams for washing away liquefied natural gas spills
    is generally
        A. *recommended*, chiefly because both practices are use-
           ful for minimizing the potential of ignition
        B. *not recommended* in the case of solid streams being
           used to wash away spills, because the rate of
           vaporization will be increased
        C. *recommended* in the case of water sprays being used
           for controlling the path of travel of vapors,
           because air entrained in the spray may create an
           explosive mixture
        D. *not recommended* in the case of either water sprays
           or solid streams, because of the increased likeli-
           hood of ignition resulting from both practices

18.___

19. Bulk liquefied petroleum gas tanks are best protected
    by a fixed water system.
    The one of the following which the water spray generally
    will NOT accomplish in the event of an exposure fire is
    to
        A. dilute the gas escaping from the tank and assist in
           producing a gas-air mixture too lean to burn
        B. cool the tank and keep the vapor pressure of the
           gas down
        C. form a mixture with the spilled liquid that will
           not ignite because the flash point will be depressed
        D. prevent localized heating of the tank sheel above
           the liquid level

19.___

20. At a fire in the electrical equipment room in the sub-cellar of a high-rise office building, a sign on the door indicates that equipment is carrying 15,000 volts. All the available Class C extinguishers have been used. The burning insulation is still giving off large volumes of smoke and gases.
Of the following, the MOST appropriate tactic generally is to

    A. operate a solid stream using a 1 1/8" tip, from a distance of at least 20 feet from the equipment
    B. operate a spray nozzle stream from a distance no closer than 6 inches from the equipment
    C. operate alternately with a combination solid stream and spray nozzle
    D. use no water unless so directed by a chief officer

20.___

KEY (CORRECT ANSWERS)

1.	D	11.	B
2.	D	12.	C
3.	C	13.	C
4.	D	14.	A
5.	A	15.	D
6.	C	16.	D
7.	D	17.	B
8.	A	18.	A
9.	B	19.	C
10.	A	20.	B

EXAMINATION SECTION

TEST 1

DIRECTIONS: Each question or incomplete statement is followed by several suggested answers or completions. Select the one that BEST answers the question or completes the statement. *PRINT THE LETTER OF THE CORRECT ANSWER IN THE SPACE AT THE RIGHT.*

1. While supervising an inspection of a commercial building,   1.___
   an officer notices some wooden packing cases resting
   against a steam riser.
   He advises the owner to move the stock at least 12 inches
   away from the riser to permit air to circulate.
   This advice generally is
   A. *proper*; however, a clearance of 36 inches should have
      been suggested
   B. *improper*; steam risers do not reach the ignition
      temperature of wood
   C. *proper*; standard practice uses a rise of 90°F above
      room temperature as the maximum permissible tempera-
      ture on surrounding woodwork
   D. *improper*; the air space suggested may permit hidden
      fire to travel behind the stock

2. A chauffeur of a fire apparatus enroute to a fire removes   2.___
   his foot from the accelerator pedal as he approaches an
   intersection and holds it poised above the brake pedal.
   This chauffeur's action generally is
   A. *proper*, chiefly because the apparatus will slow down
      gradually and safely
   B. *improper*, chiefly because he cannot accelerate rapid-
      ly if necessary to pull away from a potential
      accident
   C. *proper*, chiefly because stopping distance is reduced
      if it is necessary to stop suddenly
   D. *improper*, chiefly because he is unnecessarily delay-
      ing the response to the fire

3. The one of the following which is NOT a correct statement   3.___
   concerning operations at fires in tenements is that
   A. when an apartment has two doors it is best to force
      the door normally used for entrance
   B. smoke issuing from the cornice is positive evidence
      that fire has entered the cockloft
   C. a count of the number of mail boxes on each wall of
      the building entrance hall can indicate the number
      of apartments per floor
   D. secondary searches of an area should be performed by
      members other than those who performed the primary
      search in the area

4. The command *Lift* followed by the command *Load* is MOST
   appropriate for use when the operation involves

   A. loading a victim on a stretcher into an ambulance
   B. loading a victim onto a stretcher using four bearers
   C. loading a victim onto a stretcher using eight bearers
   D. lowering a victim in a Stokes stretcher

   4.___

5. At a fire in a warehouse protected by an ablative water
   system, it is MOST likely that

   A. less water is needed than with a conventional sprink-
      ler system
   B. more water is needed than with a conventional sprink-
      ler system
   C. small hose lines will not be needed for mop-up opera-
      tions
   D. heavy hose streams will be needed to flush out the
      warehouse making the fire area visible

   5.___

6. It has been suggested that when a portable ladder is
   raised to effect immediate roof ventilation at a taxpayer fire, another ladder should be raised at the other
   end of the taxpayer.
   Of the following, the MAIN reason for raising this second
   ladder is to

   A. provide a means of access for hose lines
   B. provide an alternate escape route to members on the
      roof
   C. indicate the fire building to incoming fire personnel
   D. allow more truckmen to gain access to the roof

   6.___

7. The one of the following statements concerning the Stang
   Intelligent Nozzle that is NOT correct is that the

   A. use of the 2" tip is restricted to the fixed (pumper)
      position
   B. nozzle cannot be lowered below 25° above horizontal
   C. member controlling the stream shall stand on the
      platform when the nozzle is in portable position
   D. siamese is positioned at the front for supply hose
      lines when the nozzle is mounted on the pumper

   7.___

8. When using a master stream fog nozzle on a ladder pipe
   and the ladder is extended over 65 feet, nozzle pressure,
   in psi, is NOT to exceed

   A. 60   B. 70   C. 80   D. 90

   8.___

9. While working at a fire with Scott Air-Pak donned, an
   officer occasionally removes a glove from his hand and
   seems to feel about and overhead in the air.
   The actions of this officer are

   A. *proper*, primarily because he will be more aware of
      hazardous objects in the area
   B. *improper*, primarily because he is exposing himself
      to nails, glass, and other sharp objects

   9.___

C. *proper*, primarily because he is better able to feel temperature conditions in the area

D. *improper*, primarily because he is setting a bad example for the men he is leading

10. The one of the following which is NOT a correct statement with respect to the company handi-talkie radio is that 10.___
   A. if the handi-talkie becomes wet at operations it is to be stored in a flat position when drying
   B. in some sections of the city only three of the six frequencies can be used
   C. when the green lamp glows and the red lamp goes out, the battery charger has fully charged the battery
   D. the primary command channel is restricted to use by chief officers at an expanding operation

11. At a fire at the top of a 30-story building with a spacing of 19 feet between floors, the engine company chauffeur supplies a pressure of 300 pounds to the standpipe. 11.___
   Of the following, it would be MOST appropriate to describe this action as
   A. *incorrect*, mainly because only five pounds per floor is needed to overcome head loss
   B. *correct*, mainly because a pressure of over 200 pounds is needed to overcome head loss
   C. *incorrect*, mainly because fire department hose is tested at only 300 pounds
   D. *correct*, mainly because this pressure is needed to overcome friction loss in the hose at high elevations

12. The flammability limits of aviation fuels are of little significance in understanding their fire hazard properties CHIEFLY because the fuels 12.___
   A. have practically the same limits
   B. form flammable vapor-air mixtures at all temperatures
   C. ignite readily under tank failure conditions
   D. resist flashing to vapor when in the gelled form

13. External cardiac massage should be stopped for no more than five seconds during the administration of cardio-pulmonary resuscitation. 13.___
   The only one of the following which is an acceptable reason for such a stoppage is to
   A. administer an appropriate rescue breathing cycle
   B. determine whether pulse has spontaneously returned
   C. defibrillate the heart with a sharp blow
   D. replace one rescuer with another

14. According to Kimball, on a first alarm, one adequately manned response group (two engines, one truck) is normally expected to be able to efficiently apply, from properly deployed hand lines, *between* _____ and _____ gpm. 14.___
   A. 200; 300   B. 400; 500   C. 600; 700   D. 800; 1000

15. The number of sprinkler heads that can be effectively supplied through a fire department connection by a 1000 gpm pumper operating at 100 to 150 lbs/sq.in. is generally considered to be MOST NEARLY

    A. 50   B. 100   C. 150   D. 200   15.___

16. When using 2½" hose and FT-1 (Fog Tip) with plain water, an increase in nozzle pressure from 85 psi to 95 psi, all other factors remaining equal, will yield an increased flow, in gallons per minute, of MOST NEARLY

    A. 10   B. 25   C. 50   D. 75   16.___

17. According to the regulations, the particulars of a false alarm and arrest shall be promptly telephoned to the office of the chief of department.
The officer responsible for this notification is the
    A. battalion chief who ordered the arrest
    B. officer on duty in the unit of the department witness
    C. officer on duty in whose district the box is located
    D. battalion chief in whose district the box is located   17.___

18. According to the regulations, company commanders shall cause a thorough inspection of all schools within their administrative district.
Such inspections shall be made
    A. annually
    B. semi-annually
    C. at the beginning of each school term
    D. within 60 days after school opens for the fall term   18.___

19. When members require medical treatment as a result of respiratory injuries with masks, the masks or cylinders involved shall be impounded by the officer in command and forwarded for analysis to the
    A. medical office
    B. bureau of fire investigation
    C. division of training
    D. bureau of personnel and administration   19.___

20. According to regulations, when covering captains are available, division fire prevention coordinators shall utilize them for the purpose of
    A. inspection of target hazards
    B. inspection of public assembly occupancies
    C. performing field inspection duty in units with a backlog of inspections
    D. relieving assigned captains on duty to perform field inspection duty within their administrative districts   20.___

KEY (CORRECT ANSWERS)

1.	C	11.	B
2.	C	12.	C
3.	B	13.	B
4.	A	14.	B
5.	A	15.	A
6.	B	16.	C
7.	B	17.	B
8.	D	18.	A
9.	C	19.	C
10.	A	20.	D

TEST 2

DIRECTIONS: Each question or incomplete statement is followed by several suggested answers or completions. Select the one that BEST answers the question or completes the statement. *PRINT THE LETTER OF THE CORRECT ANSWER IN THE SPACE AT THE RIGHT.*

1. The need for extensive overhauling in severely damaged buildings may be *obviated* when emergency command procedures are in effect by
    A. vacating the buildings
    B. deluging the buildings with heavy streams
    C. permitting fire to burn out all combustible contents
    D. arranging for the demolition of the buildings

1.___

2. If apparatus has not received an annual safety check, a report shall be forwarded to the chief in charge, division of repairs and transportation, by the
    A. company commander
    B. battalion commander
    C. division commander
    D. assistant or deputy assistant chief

2.___

3. Hose lines stretched in the street to prevent involvement of adjacent properties at manhole fires *should* be positioned at points
    A. beyond the predictable limits of fire or explosion damage
    B. such that they can reach each manhole involved in fire
    C. allowing coverage both of the manholes and the adjacent properties
    D. where the electric feed lines enter the adjacent properties

3.___

4. The one of the following which is NOT generally a correct statement with respect to operations on track areas of subways and railroads is that
    A. trains will operate in both directions on the same track at very close time intervals on railroads other than the transit authority
    B. members ordered to halt traffic, when attempting to stop a train, shall move their lights in a vigorous back and forth motion
    C. all under-river tunnels of the transit authority are equipped with standpipes that are city main connected at each end and protected from freezing
    D. when power in a section of track is removed, the subway motorman is expected to coast into the next station to allow the safest method of passenger unloading

4.___

5. Assume that there are two pieces of apparatus in the same company and both respond to an alarm. Of the following statements, the one that is CORRECT regarding this situation is that
    A. six men can adequately man both pieces of equipment
    B. five-man manning shall apply to both pieces of equipment
    C. three men shall respond on the first piece of equipment and two on the second piece of equipment
    D. five-man manning shall apply only to the primary piece of equipment

5.___

6. According to the guidelines for making group changes, all group changes shall be approved by
    A. company commanders for firemen, battalion commanders for lieutenants, and division commanders for captains
    B. battalion commanders for firemen and division commanders for covering and covering relief officers
    C. battalion commanders for firemen for covering and covering relief lieutenants and division commanders for covering and covering relief captains
    D. battalion chiefs for firemen and deputy chiefs for covering and covering relief officers

6.___

7. The one of the following statements which is NOT correct with respect to the multiversal nozzle and its use is that a multiversal nozzle lashed to a
    A. portable ladder is of particular value from elevated positions at the rear and sides of buildings
    B. 15' truss ladder is permitted to be moved by horizontal or vertical movement of the ladder
    C. portable ladder should not be dragged to another position without shutting down its supply
    D. 15' truss ladder may not be supplied by hose larger than 3"

7.___

8. Of the following statements concerning the control and accountability for paychecks distributed to units, the one which is INACCURATE is that
    A. more than one initial may appear opposite a name
    B. an officer receiving checks shall enter his initials in the remarks column of the payroll opposite each name for which he distributes a check
    C. the last initial appearing to the right indicates the officer accountable for custody, distribution, or return of that check
    D. a relieving officer shall place his initial in the remarks column of the payroll opposite each name for which he issues a check

8.___

9. Of the following, the FINAL step a fireman may take to   9.___
resolve a grievance after all his appeals have failed
is to
    A. ask the union to bring his grievance to the impar-
       tial chairman for arbitration
    B. inform the division commander of his grievance within
       five days after he has received the latest determina-
       tion on his appeal
    C. send a report to the fire commissioner on the pre-
       scribed form for grievances
    D. tell the president and members of the executive
       board of the union about his grievance and let
       them take action

10. When a violation order is to be served and the owner or   10.___
person in charge of the premises cannot readily be
located, every effort shall be made to serve such order.
Of the following statements concerning the attempts to
serve such an order, the one that is NOT correct is:
    A. Attempt to ascertain from occupants or people in
       area the name and address of the owner or manage-
       ment
    B. Send a member to effect service if the owner or
       management is located in the city but out of the
       company district
    C. Make an appointment by telephone for service of the
       order
    D. Post the violation notice prominently in or on the
       premises and mail a copy to the owner or management

11. Every applicant for a certificate of license to install   11.___
underground gasoline storage tanks is required to
    A. be a resident of the city and maintain a place of
       business in the city
    B. file a bond and evidence of liability insurance
    C. be a resident of the city or maintain a place of
       business in the city
    D. pass a written examination given by the Fire Depart-
       ment

12. The Fire Prevention Code specifies that a special permit   12.___
is required for each of the following EXCEPT
    A. refining petroleum collected from oil separators
       or manufacturing plants
    B. loading of small arms ammunition by hand in a retail
       store selling ammunition
    C. operating a wholesale drug or chemical house
    D. generating acetylene gas

13. The one of the following that is the MOST acceptable   13.___
statement concerning the fire protection for the truck
loading rack in a bulk oil terminal is that the rack
must be equipped with a _____ system, _____ controlled.
    A. water spray; automatically
    B. foam; remote manually
    C. water spray; remote manually
    D. foam; automatically

14. The one of the following which is NOT in accord with the   14.___
    regulations for the use of Halon 1301, extinguishing
    agent, is that
    A. maximum concentration shall not exceed 10 percent
       where human habitation is present in the volume to
       be flooded
    B. minimum concentration of FE 1301 used shall not be
       less than 10 percent
    C. a discharge rate which results in attaining the
       design concentration in 8 seconds is acceptable
    D. a central office connection must be provided for
       fire detection or systems operation where human
       habitation is present in the volume to be flooded

15. At a fire in a high-rise office building equipped with   15.___
    a stair pressurization system, the MAXIMUM number of
    doors in the stair shaft that can be opened without
    concern about reducing the pressure differential below
    design limits is
    A. *two*, the door to the fire floor and the one immedi-
       ately below
    B. *three*, the door to the fire floor and two others
    C. *four*, the door to the fire floor and the three doors
       below the fire floor level
    D. *five*, the door to the fire floor and the doors at
       the two levels above and below the fire floor

16. A captain responds to a fire under a pier on which baled   16.___
    sisal is normally handled. There are openings in the
    deck, for revolving nozzles.
    If the installation is in accordance with Fire Department
    regulations, these openings would be found
    A. in the center of each firestopped area
    B. at the longitudinal center line of the pier at 50-
       foot intervals
    C. across the pier at 100-foot intervals with not over
       50 feet between openings in a transverse direction
    D. at 25-foot intervals longitudinally and transversely

17. The one of the following which is NOT required by the   17.___
    housing maintenance code for the protection of openings
    into public halls in old-law tenements less than four
    stories high is that *every*
    A. door opening into a public hall shall be fireproof,
       having a fire-resisting rating of at least one hour
    B. door opening into the public hall shall be self-
       closing
    C. glazed panel in a door opening into a public hall
       shall be glazed with wire glass
    D. transom opening upon any public hall shall be glazed
       with wire glass and firmly secured in a closed
       position

18. Firestopping of the space above a hung ceiling into areas   18.___
    not exceeding 3000 square feet is *required* when the
    A. structural members within the concealed space are
       individually protected with materials having the
       required fire resistance
    B. concealed space is sprinklered
    C. ceiling contributes to the required fire resistance
       of the floor or roof assembly
    D. ceiling is not an essential part of the fire-
       resistive assembly

19. When a deluge sprinkler system is provided around the   19.___
    perimeter of a theater stage, manual operating devices
    as well as automatic controls are required by the
    building code.
    The MOST complete and accurate statement concerning these
    manual operating devices is that they should be located
    A. at the emergency control station
    B. adjacent to one exit from the stage
    C. at the emergency control station and adjacent to one
       exit from the stage
    D. at the emergency control station, adjacent to one
       exit from the stage, and at the deluge valve

20. Yellow painted siamese caps on office buildings will   20.___
    indicate that the siamese serves *only*
    A. the standpipe in pressurized stairs
    B. the sprinklers in sub-basement locations
    C. a combination standpipe and sprinkler system
    D. as a supply line to the fire pump for the upper level
       standpipe outlets

KEY (CORRECT ANSWERS)

1. A		11. C	
2. C		12. D	
3. A		13. C	
4. C		14. B	
5. D		15. B	
6. B		16. D	
7. D		17. A	
8. D		18. C	
9. A		19. C	
10. D		20. C	

EXAMINATION SECTION
TEST 1

DIRECTIONS: Each question or incomplete statement is followed by several suggested answers or completions. Select the one that BEST answers the question or completes the statement. *PRINT THE LETTER OF THE CORRECT ANSWER IN THE SPACE AT THE RIGHT.*

1. Assume that you are in command of the second ladder company   1.___
   to arrive at a medium fire situation in an occupied,
   detached, private dwelling during the early morning hours.
   Of the following, your PRIMARY objective should be to
   A. augment the search for life and then assist as needed
   B. assure complete roof ventilation and removal of such
      items as glass, sash, curtains, and blinds to facili-
      tate the inside operation
   C. have your inside team prepared to engage in mask
      operations
   D. examine shrubbery under open windows and porch roofs
      for persons who may have jumped prior to your arrival

2. A considerable number of serious burn injuries and fatali-   2.___
   ties result from fires involving clothing being worn. The
   following may or may not be correct statements concerning
   fire department experience gained from such fires:
   I. Cotton and rayon have proved to be relatively non-
      flammable fibers
   II. Nylon and acetate melt and liquefy under fire expo-
      sure, thereby tending to aggravate the severity of
      burn injuries
   III. Victims of clothing fires are more likely to be
      persons over 60 years of age than children under 10
   Which of the following choices contains only those of the
   above-mentioned statements that are generally CORRECT?
   A. I, II   B. I, III
   C. II, III   D. I, II, III

3. A large building has smoke coming out the eaves, cracks   3.___
   around doors and windows, and other openings in the
   structure. This situation signals *backdraft possible*.
   The one of the following actions which is MOST likely to
   reduce the possibility of a backdraft under these condi-
   tions is to
   A. position heavy streams around the building
   B. ventilate the building from the lower floors up
   C. start venting gases from the roof when lines are
      positioned and ready
   D. open up the roof when a line is positioned to direct
      its stream down into fire coming from the roof opening

4. When fire heavily involves several floors of a building,   4.___
   the one of the following that is the LEAST appropriate
   way to operate a tower ladder stream is to
      A. start at the lower fire level and work upward to in-
          sure the safety of the members operating above the
          fire
      B. position the nozzle close to and low in the window to
          avoid exposing members to escaping heat
      C. increase the nozzle pressure within allowable limits
          to attempt partition and sidewall penetration
      D. position the basket, when building wall stability is
          in doubt, so its horizontal distance from the building
          wall is at least 1/3 its vertical distance from the
          top of the wall

5. Because of ineffectiveness or danger to personnel, water   5.___
   as a fire suppression agent in any form should NOT
   generally be used on fires involving
      A. flammable liquids
      B. sodium metal
      C. live electrical equipment
      D. combustible dusts

6. When firefighters and other emergency personnel fight   6.___
   chemical fires involving pesticides, the severity of the
   emergency can be compounded by inappropriate action.
   The one of the following that is generally the MOST appropriate practice for avoiding aggravated emergencies is to
      A. flood the fire with straight streams
      B. detoxify the chemicals by attacking the fire with fog
          nozzles in the spray position
      C. allow the pesticides already involved in fire to burn
          if extinguishment will not save the building
      D. evacuate civilians and attack the fire from downwind

7. LEXAN is a polycarbonate glazing material used to replace   7.___
   glass in high security and vandalism areas. LEXAN windows,
   as presently installed, are generally very difficult to
   ventilate.
   Of the following, it would be LEAST appropriate to state
   that, where LEXAN is encountered,
      A. using conventional forcible entry tools, including
          the pike head axe, is ineffective
      B. it might be possible to use a portable ladder to push
          a ground level LEXAN window inward
      C. it may be best to remove the window framing or mul-
          lions rather than attack the LEXAN
      D. the Superior Air Hammer (air chisel) with the carbide-
          tipped blade may be effective but slow

8. The chimney effect that occurs at tenement dumbwaiter   8.___
   fires allows heat and smoke to rise rapidly to the upper
   floors and roof space.

Of the following engine company tactics, the one that is
generally MOST appropriate for use at the typical tenement
dumbwaiter fire is to
A. stretch enough line to reach the top floor
B. stretch enough line up the interior stairs as far as
heat and smoke conditions permit
C. start water in the line without orders as soon as
connections are made
D. allow only one member at a time to extend himself into
the shaft while fighting the fire

9. In the past, collapse of residential structures has been   9.___
rare and was usually the result of a long-burning fire,
with the collapse anticipated and safety precautions
established. In recent years, however, the vacant building, often residential, has become the most frequent scene
of collapse.
The one of the following which is generally LEAST likely
to be a significant indicator of a potential collapse in
vacant multiple dwellings is
A. sagging floors
B. numerous large holes in floors
C. runoff water
D. large pieces of plaster sliding off walls

10. Of the following methods of fire control, the one that is   10.___
LEAST likely to be effective for the extinguishment of
fires involving high concentrations of nitrates is
A. oxygen dilution
B. cooling
C. fuel removal
D. chemical flame inhibition

11. A captain preparing an outline for a drill in quarters on   11.___
the advantages and disadvantages of portable extinguishers
lists the following four items in his outline:
   I. Use of the CO_2 extinguisher is likely to cause shocks
      to the operator from the buildup of static electricity
      when the extinguisher is being discharged
  II. Dry chemical agents may clog filters of nearby air
      conditioners
 III. The use of CO_2 in a confined space may cause disori-
      entation or loss of consciousness
  IV. Plain water-type extinguishers can cause Class B fires
      to flare up and spread
Which of the following choices lists only those of the
captain's considerations which are likely to be DISADVAN-
TAGES?
   A. III, IV   B. I, II
   C. II, III, IV   D. I, II, III, IV

12. The Hurst Power Tool is described as a hydraulic spread-   12.___
ing and pulling device. The one of the following that
is generally NOT a correct statement about this tool is
that the
   A. tool can be placed into operation immediately even
      if the thumb controls have not been operated to make
      the arms move through several extension and contrac-
      tion cycles
   B. jaws should be left about one-half inch apart before
      shutting down the power unit
   C. arms will retain their bite during power unit failure
      even if the thumb control triggers are manipulated
   D. thumb controls move in the same direction as the
      arms (out to open, in to close) if the hoses have
      been made up correctly

13. The one of the following actions which is MOST appropriate   13.___
for the officer in command of an incendiary fire to take
is to
   A. question a person who is loitering suspiciously at
      the scene
   B. arrest someone who has admitted setting the fire
   C. forbid an individual who has witnessed the act of
      arson to leave the scene
   D. instruct all persons offering information about a
      perpetrator to await the arrival of the fire marshal

14. The construction of oil tankers typically includes coffer-   14.___
dams. Of the following, it would generally be LEAST
appropriate for the company officer to assume that coffer-
dams on oil tankers
   A. separate individual cargo oil tanks
   B. separate the engine room aft and cargo space forward
   C. consist of two watertight bulkheads, 3 to 6 feet apart
   D. have provisions to be flooded to form a fire break

15. During the course of a first-aid drill, a company officer   15.___
makes the following statements to the members. The one
of the following statements which conveys generally
INACCURATE information to the members is:
   A. The triangular bandage is useful as an emergency
      cover for the entire scalp, the hand or foot.
      Folded into a cravat (necktie) bandage, the triangle
      can be used as a circular, spiral or figure-eight
      bandage
   B. Elastic bandages are the most difficult to apply; if
      too tight, they may cause some impairment of circula-
      tion, but they won't impair nerve function
   C. If the patient complains of numbness or a tingling
      sensation, the bandage should be loosened immediately
   D. Never apply a wet gauze bandage as a tight circular
      bandage about a person's neck

16. Before leaving quarters to perform apparatus field
inspection duty (A.F.I.D.) at a hospital, a company
officer holds a drill on institutional fire safety.
It would be MOST appropriate for the officer to tell the
members that the majority of fires in hospitals generally
occur in

    A. storage rooms   B. lounges
    C. patients' rooms   D. corridors

16.___

17. Improper parking of fire apparatus at the scene of fires,
emergencies, and field inspection activities has contri-
buted to vehicular accidents and personal injuries.
The one of the following precautions that generally is
MOST valid is:

    A. When necessary to double-park apparatus on a one-way
       street against the flow of traffic, park on your
       left side of the street
    B. Repositioning of angle-parked and double-parked appa-
       ratus should be accomplished as soon as practicable
       by qualified personnel of units leaving the scene of
       operations
    C. When inspections are being made on a narrow, dead-end
       street, apparatus may be operated in reverse and
       backed into the street so as to be parked facing the
       direction of response
    D. While on A.F.I.D., avoid angle parking, double park-
       ing, or parking alongside building materials at
       construction sites; when visibility is poor, use
       spaces near hydrants and use emergency flasher lights
       to alert other drivers

17.___

18. In order for a company commander to maintain a high level
of inspectional skill and provide motivation for members,
special drill lectures shall be prepared. Each of the
following points should be emphasized during these lectures EXCEPT the

    A. problems of illegal occupancies and the need for
       verification of the certificate of occupancy
    B. need for completeness and accuracy in the preparation
       of fire prevention inspectional forms and documents
    C. necessity of issuing sufficient violation orders to
       justify the fire prevention program
    D. basis for sprinkler recommendations in buildings

18.___

19. Knowledge of extinguishment procedures, including the
use of water in its various forms and extinguishment
agents, is essential if fires involving the different
types of magnesium are to be handled correctly.
The one of the following statements concerning the extinguishment of magnesium fires that is LEAST appropriate is:

    A. Hot magnesium reacts with water, liberating hydrogen,
       but the danger of a hydrogen explosion under fire
       conditions is generally slight

19.___

B. Dry chemical extinguishers containing sodium bicarbonate may be used on magnesium since they are effective in reducing the burning rate and are non-reactive
C. Magnesium fires can be extinguished with water by cooling the metal below its melting point but large amounts of water may be needed
D. Water trapped below the surface of molten metal, as might occur if a solid stream were directed into it, will produce a much greater eruption effect than will water sprayed on the surface and turned to steam without confinement

20. A company commander, instructing members in procedures   20.___
    to be followed in court appearances involving false-alarm
    responses, states that the following are facts to which
    a member may be appropriately required to testify for a
    conviction to be obtained:
      I. The box, time, and date that the alarm was transmitted
     II. The number of units who responded to the alarm
    III. That a diligent search at the scene was made
     IV. That there was no fire or emergency
    Which of the following choices lists ALL of the above
    statements that a testifying member should know?
      A. I, II, and III, but not IV
      B. II, III, and IV, but not I
      C. I, III, and IV, but not II
      D. I, II, III, and IV

———

KEY (CORRECT ANSWERS)

1. A		11. D	
2. C		12. C	
3. C		13. B	
4. D		14. A	
5. B		15. B	
6. C		16. C	
7. D		17. C	
8. C		18. C	
9. C		19. B	
10. A		20. D	

———

TEST 2

DIRECTIONS: Each question or incomplete statement is followed by several suggested answers or completions. Select the one that BEST answers the question or completes the statement. *PRINT THE LETTER OF THE CORRECT ANSWER IN THE SPACE AT THE RIGHT.*

1. A truck company officer leads his men in performing forcible entry, search, ventilation, and overhauling operations at a fire in a third-floor apartment of a six-story building. During these operations, this officer makes the following observations:
   I. The stairway to the fire apartment is blocked by boxes and crates on the second-floor landing
   II. His company, the first to arrive, is promptly directed to the fire apartment by a resident of an apartment neighboring on the fire apartment
   III. There appears to be one point of fire origin in the apartment
   IV. Runoff water has a brownish color and dry ash on charred furniture is shiny black

   Which of the following choices lists only those observations that generally should cause the officer to believe that the fire was of suspicious origin?
   A. I, III   B. I, IV   C. II, III   D. II, IV

2. Assume that you are the newly-assigned commanding officer of an engine company with a poor accident record. In developing a corrective action program, it would be LEAST appropriate for you to state to your chauffeurs:
   A. When driving a pumper, a defensive driver *squares* his turns because he is aware of the length of his apparatus and the resultant fact that the rear wheels track inside the front wheels
   B. *Parking on air* refers to the use of the Maxibrake as a parking brake, which provides the safest of all parking brakes in vehicles equipped with an air brake system. It is not to be confused with the Tractor Protection Valve, which should not be used as a parking brake but provides positive mechanical application of brakes through a safety chamber and compressed powerful spring
   C. *Fanning* an air brake pedal, just as pumping a hydraulic brake pedal, may be required to regain lost traction due to a skid
   D. Parking on a steep grade necessitates tightening the adjusting knob on the Ausolon parking brake to a point where extraordinary effort is required to bring the lever over center

3. Manila rope is at its maximum strength when the strain from a load is applied to all fibers alike. When a knot is tied in a length of rope, the weakest point is at the knot. The strength loss will vary according to the knot used.
   Of the following knots, the one which can generally cause the GREATEST strength loss is the
   A. square knot   B. bowline
   C. clove hitch   D. short splice

3.___

4. While on housewatch duty, a fireman becomes ill. The man's symptoms are persistent pain in the chest, shoulders, and left arm, and he is experiencing shortness of breath. His company officer, also observing that the fireman is pale and his lips are bluish, immediately relieves him from housewatch duty.
   Which of the following would NOT be an appropriate step for the officer to take?
   A. Have the medical officer on duty called before transporting the fireman to a hospital
   B. Start mouth-to-mouth respiration, even though the victim is breathing
   C. Call for an ambulance equipped with oxygen
   D. Place the man in a comfortable, sitting-up position

4.___

5. Of the following guidelines relating to control techniques and extinguishing agents to be used at liquefied natural gas (LNG) fires, the one that is generally MOST appropriate is:
   A. LNG vapors may be made more buoyant, assisting in moving vapors away from ignition sources, by warming the vapors with a spray stream of water
   B. High expansion foam, properly applied to a pool of LNG will float, partially freeze, and, thereby, seal the vapors below
   C. LNG fires may actually be intensified by the decomposition of halogenated hydrocarbons used as an extinguishing agent
   D. Water is unable to effectively extinguish LNG fires and it is, therefore, precluded from use in the control of these fires

5.___

6. Assume that you are a captain leading the first-arriving company at an emergency scene at a high-rise apartment building. You discover that the elevator, which has center-opening doors, has plunged from the top floor of the building and stalled suddenly at approximately, the tenth-floor level. Each of the six passengers is conscious and able to move, but incapacitated to the extent of not being able to assist rescuers to force the elevator door open.
   In taking the necessary steps to rescue these passengers, the one of the following that would be MOST advisable for you to do is to

6.___

    A. order that the main line switch be left on, but in-
       struct one of the passengers to place the *Stop* switch
       in the *OFF* position
    B. instruct the passengers to move, three to each side
       of the cab, and sit down facing the perimeter of the
       cab
    C. order the power turned off and try to pass a hook to
       the hoistway interlock from the floor above
    D. ask the passengers to move close to the doors to be
       prepared for immediate exit when the doors are opened

7. Bulk-storage tanks with floating roofs are designed to   7.___
   reduce fire hazards in storing flammable liquids.
   Which of the following statements concerning this type
   of tank is generally CORRECT?
    A. Fires above the floating roof surface are most effec-
       tively controlled by application of high expansion
       foam.
    B. When there is a fire involving a covered floating
       roof tank, the recommended method of extinguishment
       is subsurface injection of fluoroprotein foam through
       the vents of the floating roof.
    C. Regardless of fire extinguishment conditions, the
       floating roof will remain afloat and will continue
       to give satisfactory service.
    D. When there is a fire involving the seal of a floating
       roof, firemen can fight it in routine fashion by
       climbing the tank stairs and applying foam from hand-
       lines.

8. During a drill on gas installations, a captain makes the   8.___
   following statements:
    I. If the shutoff valve is in line with the pipe, the
      gas is on.
    II. When black smoke is emitting from a gas meter after
      the gas is shut off, the fire may be extinguished.
   III. Once a meter is shut off by fire department personnel,
      it should only be turned on by gas company personnel.
    IV. The gas supply in a burning building should not be
      turned off if the fire is remote from the meter.
   The one of the following choices that lists ALL of the
   above statements that are generally CORRECT is:
    A. I
    B. I and II
    C. I, II, and III
    D. I, II, III, and IV

9. As a result of a split casing and damaged inner tank, oil   9.___
   escapes from a large electrical transformer, ignites and
   involves the transformer in fire. Of the following, it
   would generally be LEAST appropriate in this situation to
   use ladder pipes operating in the fog position and, from
   a distance, to

A. protect firefighters from explosions or further vessel failure
B. guard against electrocution if power has not been turned off
C. reduce the flames so foam handlines can move closer to the fire
D. provide additional cooling to augment a foam attack

10. Assume that you are a captain in command of a company. You arrive first in response to an alarm of a fire in a high-rise building and note smoke pushing out of the exterior skin of the building about the fifteenth floor. The one of the following actions which you should take at this point is to
    A. determine the location of the fire service elevator
    B. transmit a second alarm
    C. order a member with a handie-talkie to the fire floor to investigate and report back to you
    D. proceed to the fire floor with the company via elevator

10.___

11. The difficulties encountered in fighting fire in the cellar of a pool supply occupancy were compounded by bulk storage of calcium hypochlorite. This bleaching and sanitizing agent is LEAST likely to
    A. be unstable and highly combustible when finely divided
    B. form a mixture that spontaneously bursts into flame on contact with oxidizable material
    C. decompose when involved in fire, by liberating oxygen and intensifying the fire
    D. have an increased fire and explosion potential when pre-mixed with algaecides and fungicides as an all-purpose water treatment

11.___

12. Acetylene is a particularly hazardous flammable gas because, in addition to its flammability, it is reactive and unstable. Consequently, its storage and handling in some respects differs from other flammable gases.
The following statements may be pertinent to acetylene and its storage:
    I. Acetylene is not toxic, but can have an anesthetic effect
    II. Copper must be avoided in most acetylene piping and equipment
    III. Acetylene gas can explode if subjected to more than 15 psi.
Which one of the following choices lists only those of the above-mentioned statements that are generally CORRECT?
    A. I, II   B. II, III   C. I, III   D. I, II, III

12.___

13. Assume that, as the commanding officer of a ladder company with an above-normal injury rate, you have prepared and are presenting a drill on *lifting*. You have chosen the 3" siamese fitting as the object to be lifted for demonstration.

13.___

Which of the following positions should NOT be applied, as a basic step, to safe lifting?
A. Feet parted comfortably, astride the object, and facing in the proposed direction of movement
B. Back straight, nearly vertical, and fairly rigid to avoid forming an arc
C. Object gripped with the whole hand to provide a more secure hold and to prevent undue pressure at the ends of the digits
D. Chin tucked in to straighten the whole spine, not merely the back

14. Of the following guidelines which might be applied to the utilization of elevators in a high-rise commercial building during a fire, the one which is generally MOST appropriate to use is to
A. load no more firefighters aboard an elevator than the listed capacity
B. transport members in the service elevator where available
C. direct a flashlight upwards through the hatch cover before leaving the elevator to determine conditions in the shaft
D. unload members on the floor below the fire, never on the fire floor

14.___

15. Of the following, it would be LEAST appropriate to state that double-bottom tanks on oil-fired cargo vessels
A. are at the extreme bottom of the ship and run nearly the whole length of the vessel
B. vary in depth from approximately $2\frac{1}{2}$' to 6'
C. may be subdivided into watertight compartments to carry ballast, fresh water, boiler-feed water, as well as fuel oil
D. are recommended means of emergency access to the engine room

15.___

16. The discharge of rapid water through 1 3/4" hose equipped with nozzles normally used with $2\frac{1}{2}$" hose requires changes in conventional nozzle handling techniques. The one of the following which BEST explains why the situation described requires such changes is that, generally, there is a(n)
A. excessive nozzle reaction when rapid water is used in a 1 3/4" hose line equipped with a nozzle designed for use with a $2\frac{1}{2}$" hose line
B. much reduced nozzle reaction for a given nozzle discharging the same amount of water from a 1 3/4" hose line as from a $2\frac{1}{2}$" hose line
C. much larger nozzle reaction for a given nozzle discharging the same amount of water from a 1 3/4" hose line as from a $2\frac{1}{2}$" hose line
D. greater degree of flexibility in a 1 3/4" hose line under pressure than there is in a $2\frac{1}{2}$" hose line discharging the same amount of water

16.___

17. Which one of the following hydraulic laws governing friction in hose and pipe, or examples of their application, is INCORRECT?

    A. Friction loss in hose varies directly as the length of the line provided all other conditions are equal; i.e., the friction loss in 500' of hose will be 5 times the friction loss in 100' of hose.

    B. In the same size hose, friction loss varies approximately as the square of the flow velocity; i.e., if flow velocity is quadrupled, the friction loss becomes 16 times as much.

    C. For the same discharge, friction loss varies inversely as the fifth power of the diameter of the hose; i.e., if the discharge remains the same but the size of the hose is tripled, the friction loss is 1/9 of the original friction loss.

    D. For a given flow velocity, the friction loss in the hose is approximately the same, no matter what the water pressure may be; i.e., if water velocity is 10 linear feet per second, friction loss is the same whether the pressure is 100 psi or 150 psi.

17.___

18. High expansion foam sometimes provides the way out of a difficult fire problem when the area is enclosed. The entire volume can be filled with such foam.

For firefighters, the following are some guidelines that may be appropriate when entering after an area is so filled:

    I. It is possible that products of combustion went into the make-up of the bubbles, and breathing may be hazardous.

    II. Personnel should wear self-contained breathing apparatus and employ a lifeline when entering because loss of vision may introduce injury hazards.

    III. As back-up protection, a dry chemical portable extinguisher should be taken along in the event a severe pocket of flame is encountered.

Which of the following choices contains only the above-mentioned statements that are generally CORRECT?

    A. I, II   B. II, III   C. I, III   D. I, II, III

18.___

19. Special fire hazards in industry are sometimes diminished by automatic carbon dioxide fixed-pipe extinguishing systems. While difficult to check an existing system for compliance with design and installation standards, certain of the following conditions can be noted during a building inspection to determine whether it is apparently operative and in good order:

    I. Have cylinders been weighed within the past five years and is there a visible record of such weighing?

    II. Are automatic-closing doors and shutters unobstructed and free to close upon actuation?

    III. Are there means accessible during a fire of manually actuating the system?

19.___

Which of the following choices contains only those of the above conditions that are generally VALID?
A. I, II   B. II, III   C. I, III   D. I, II, III

20. The one of the following procedures that is CORRECT when   20.____
placing a pumper in position to draft water is to
    A. make airtight all connections in the suction line to limit air leaking into the intake side of the pump
    B. make all connections and knots of the suction assembly after connecting to the inlet side of the pumper
    C. place the strainer end of the suction connection perpendicular to and well below the water surface
    D. place the pumper in position at the source of water supply so that the operating side is inboard

KEY (CORRECT ANSWERS)

1.	B	11.	A
2.	B	12.	D
3.	A	13.	A
4.	B	14.	B
5.	A	15.	D
6.	C	16.	D
7.	D	17.	C
8.	C	18.	A
9.	D	19.	B
10.	B	20.	A

TEST 3

DIRECTIONS: Each question or incomplete statement is followed by several suggested answers or completions. Select the one that BEST answers the question or completes the statement. *PRINT THE LETTER OF THE CORRECT ANSWER IN THE SPACE AT THE RIGHT.*

1. According to the regulations, officers may order use of   1.___
1 3/4" hose when compatible with fire conditions. Use of
this small-size hose line is permitted in all of the
following instances EXCEPT
   A. at pier fires
   B. in initial operations on the first floor of residence
      buildings
   C. as the initial line in standpipe operations
   D. during overhauling operations

2. According to the regulations, when responding to alarms,   2.___
sirens must be sounded with a frequency that depends on
conditions enroute. When the sirens are sounded under
these conditions, they should be operated in a fluctuating
or warbling manner.
Of the following statements, the one that is LEAST appropriate in connection with the operation of the sirens is
that
   A. a siren constantly operated at its peak, rather than
      fluctuating, will confuse civilian vehicle operators
      trying to determine the direction from which the
      apparatus is approaching
   B. the siren button should be released from time to time
      to permit the sound of sirens on other responding
      apparatus to be heard
   C. a siren sounded in a fluctuating manner as the appara-
      tus is moving between intersections will warn pedes-
      trians or vehicles pulling away from the curb
   D. the siren button should be released after the appara-
      tus has safely entered the intersection

3. A captain leading his company on apparatus field inspec-   3.___
tion duty is denied access to a building by the building
manager after presenting his identification.
Of the following actions, it would be MOST appropriate
for the captain to
   A. post an official notice of inspection on the premises
   B. notify the enforcement unit of the division of fire
      prevention
   C. give orders to have three routine inspections of
      premises made before taking special measures to gain
      access
   D. contact the building owner by telephone to request
      access

4. As a result of information that some supervisory personnel   4.___
   have offered certain inducements to their subordinates, the
   department has put all supervisory personnel on official
   notice that they may be subject to penalties for offering
   unauthorized considerations to subordinate personnel.
   Under the terms of this notice, supervisors are subject to
   any of the following penalties EXCEPT:
   A. Personal liability for any cash compensation offered
   B. Personal liability for any compensatory time offered
   C. Disciplinary action for any unauthorized inducements
      offered
   D. Pension infringements for any inducements affecting
      pension benefits

5. The one of the following actions a captain should take   5.___
   IMMEDIATELY upon finding alcoholic beverages in quarters
   is to
   A. order the medical officer on duty to the scene
   B. prefer charges against all members in quarters
   C. warn all members of their rights before questioning
      them
   D. notify the deputy chief on duty in his division

6. Commanding officers shall investigate all charges involv-   6.___
   ing members under their command and promptly forward a
   report to the division of fire control and the personnel
   division, indicating the results of such investigation.
   According to the regulations, which one of the following
   contains the MOST complete and accurate description of
   what this report should contain?
   The results of their investigation of
   A. charges and a statement as to the validity of charges
   B. charges, a statement as to the validity of charges,
      and an indication of whether such charges can be
      sustained by competent testimony
   C. charges, a statement as to the validity of charges,
      a statement as to whether such charges can be sus-
      tained by competent testimony, and the reason why
      such charges can be so sustained
   D. charges, a statement as to the validity of charges,
      a statement as to whether such charges can be sus-
      tained by competent testimony, the reason why such
      charges can be so sustained, and recommendations
      based on the conduct of the members during the past
      year

7. A company officer of an engine company is notified by the   7.___
   dispatcher that three alarm boxes on one circuit are
   inoperative. According to the manual of fire communications, the officer should
   A. cause prompt placement of *out of service* signs on
      affected boxes
   B. notify the police department

    C. cause patrols to be established to locate solid
       grounds if overhead telegraph wires are involved
    D. notify the county command and deputy chief concerned

8. During apparatus field inspection of a restaurant located   8.___
   in a building erected in 1972, a fireman finds that the
   filters for the cooking equipment exhaust system are
   cleaned every three months and the entire system is cleaned
   once a year.
   This maintenance procedure is
      A. *correct*
      B. *incorrect*, because the filters should be discarded at
         least every three months and the system cleaned at
         least once a year
      C. *incorrect*, because the filters should be discarded at
         least once a year and the system cleaned at least
         once a year
      D. *incorrect*, because both the filters and the entire
         system should be cleaned at least every three months

9. A captain tells members of his unit that, among other   9.___
   criteria, a group home is a facility for the care and
   maintenance of not less than three nor more than twelve
   children, and is classified by the building code in the
   same occupancy group as a one-family dwelling.
   This much of the definition of a group home, generally, is
      A. *correct*
      B. *incorrect*, because a group home may not have less than
         seven children
      C. *incorrect*, because a group home is for adults, not
         children
      D. *incorrect*, because a group home is classified in the
         same occupancy group as a rooming house

10. A fifty-foot high, five-story multiple dwelling built in   10.___
    1974 has a floor area of 7,000 square feet on each floor.
    It is equipped with a non-automatic dry standpipe system.
    During apparatus field inspection duty, a member discovers
    that a control valve on the standpipe is in closed posi-
    tion with no placard indicating that this was the normal
    position of the valve. Further investigation reveals that
    there is no one in the building who has a certificate of
    fitness to maintain the standpipe system.
    Of the following statements concerning the above situation,
    the one that is CORRECT is that the situation as described
    is
       A. *legal*
       B. *illegal*, because an individual with a certificate of
          fitness must be on the premises
       C. *illegal*, because an automatic system is required
       D. *illegal*, because the control valve must be in the open
          position

11. A tank truck with a capacity of 4,400 gallons is deliver-   11.___
    ing #4 fuel oil to a multiple dwelling. According to the
    specifications for tank trucks, the person in control of
    the truck and supervising this delivery
       A. *does not* require a certificate of fitness because the
          capacity of the tank is less than 5,000 gallons
       B. *does not* require a certificate of fitness because the
          tank has light oil
       C. *does not* require a certificate of fitness because the
          delivery is being made to a non-commercial occupancy
       D. *requires* a certificate of fitness because a fire
          department permit is needed for all tank trucks
          delivering #4 fuel oil

12. The multiple dwelling law states that sprinkler systems   12.___
    in lodging houses shall have a supervisory and maintenance
    service satisfactory to the fire department. The fire
    department requires a valid inspection of the sprinkler
    control valve AT LEAST once
       A. daily   B. semi-weekly
       C. weekly   D. monthly

13. Anhydrous ammonia is being used in a duplicating machine   13.___
    located in a school office. There is no one in the school
    with a certificate of fitness for the storage and use of
    ammonia or for the servicing of the duplicating machine.
    In this situation, a certificate of fitness is generally
       A. *not required*, because the machine is considered
          office equipment
       B. *not required*, unless the quantity of anhydrous ammonia
          being stored on the premises is more than two 150-lb.
          cylinders
       C. *not required*, because schools, with regular super-
          vised fire drills, are exempt from certain require-
          ments of the fire prevention code
       D. *required* whether or not a permit is needed under the
          fire prevention code

14. According to the labor law, fire drills are required to   14.___
    be conducted in certain factory buildings.
    Which of the following statements is CORRECT with respect
    to such fire drills?
       A. Fire drills are required to be conducted in every
          factory building in which there are more than 75
          persons above or below the street floor.
       B. Fire drills are not required to be conducted in
          factory buildings less than 100 feet in height.
       C. Fire drills are required to be conducted in every
          factory building over two stories in height in which
          more than twenty-five persons are employed above the
          ground floor unless the sprinkler system and number
          of occupants of the building are in accordance with
          the other provisions of the labor law.
       D. The sprinklering of a factory building is not a factor
          in determining whether or not a building is required
          to conduct fire drills.

15. A captain tells members during a drill that a red light   15.___
    and a placard should serve to locate the siamese hose
    connection of a temporary standpipe system in a building
    under construction.
    The captain's instructions are
    A. *correct*, because both the red light and a placard are
       required
    B. *incorrect*, because only the red light is required
    C. *incorrect*, because only a placard is required
    D. *incorrect*, because neither the red light nor a placard
       is required

16. During apparatus field inspection duty, a fireman inspect-   16.___
    ing a 40-story office building occupied by 1,000 people is
    unable to find a fire safety director or deputy fire safety
    director in the building. The manager of the building
    states that the fire safety director is out to lunch, that
    there is no deputy fire safety director, and that he, the
    manager, is acting as the fire safety director pending the
    return of the fire safety director. Because the manager
    does not have a fire safety director certificate of fit-
    ness, the fireman issues a violation to him.
    The fireman's action in this situation is
    A. *correct*, because local law requires a fire safety
       director with a certificate of fitness in a building
       this high to be on duty whenever the building is
       occupied by more than 500 people
    B. *incorrect*, because local law permits the fire safety
       director to be temporarily relieved, for short inter-
       vals, by responsible individuals who do not have the
       required certificate of fitness
    C. *correct*, because local law requires a fire safety
       director with a certificate of fitness to be on duty
       in a building this high regardless of the occupancy
       of the building
    D. *incorrect*, because whenever local law is not complied
       with, a referral report should be forwarded, and no
       violation issued

17. A commercial vehicle without a fire department permit is   17.___
    transporting 500 pounds of dynamite from a neighboring
    outside county through the city to another out-of-town
    county without stopping to make any deliveries enroute.
    There is no department pumping engine escort.
    The situation as described is
    A. *legal*, because the shipment contains less than 1,000
       pounds of dynamite
    B. *illegal*, because a pumping engine escort is required
       whenever explosives are transported without a fire
       department permit through the city
    C. *legal*, even though a fire department permit has not
       been issued because the shipment does not contain any
       blasting caps
    D. *illegal*, because dynamite may not be transported
       through the city from one out-of-town location to
       another

18. Of the following exit doors in buildings erected in 1976,   18.___
    the one that does NOT have to swing outward is a(n)
    A. corridor door from a room used for office purposes
       with an occupancy of 80 persons
    B. corridor door from a lecture room in a school build-
       ing where the room has an occupancy of 80 persons
    C. exterior street-floor exit door from a space 2,000
       square feet in area in a business building, where the
       space is occupied by fewer than 50 persons and the
       maximum travel distance to the door is 50 feet
    D. exterior street-floor exit door from a lobby in a
       hotel, where the lobby will not be occupied by more
       than 50 persons and the maximum travel distance to
       the door is 50 feet

19. During apparatus field inspection duty, a fireman inspect-   19.___
    ing a 90-foot high apartment house erected in 1972 finds
    that the standpipe hose is missing from every hose rack
    in the building.
    Of the following statements concerning this situation, the
    one that is CORRECT is that
    A. the situation as described may be legal but the fire-
       man needs additional information to make a final
       decision
    B. all such buildings, regardless of when erected, must
       have the standpipe hose racks equipped with hose
    C. all such buildings, if erected under the new building
       code, must have their standpipe hose racks equipped
       with hose
    D. the situation as described would be acceptable for an
       office building but not for an apartment house

20. A permit is required to store empty combustible packing   20.___
    boxes in a building whenever the
    A. boxes occupy more than two thousand cubic feet
    B. storage space is less than 50 feet from the nearest
       wall of a building occupied as a hospital, school,
       or theater
    C. boxes are of cardboard or similarly combustible
       material
    D. building is of non-fireproof construction

KEY (CORRECT ANSWERS)

1. C	6. C	11. D	16. D
2. D	7. A	12. C	17. B
3. B	8. D	13. D	18. C
4. D	9. B	14. C	19. A
5. C	10. D	15. A	20. A

EXAMINATION SECTION
TEST 1

DIRECTIONS: Each question or incomplete statement is followed by several suggested answers or completions. Select the one that BEST answers the question or completes the statement. *PRINT THE LETTER OF THE CORRECT ANSWER IN THE SPACE AT THE RIGHT.*

1. In general, the one of the following which an officer should NOT do in delegating decision-making authority is to
   A. insure that the activities of his subordinates conform to patterns of behavior consistent with organizational needs
   B. assume that his decisions may not be as good as those of his subordinates
   C. permit his subordinates to undertake whatever action they consider appropriate
   D. set the goals and let his subordinates decide how to achieve them

1. ___

2. A captain decides that there is a need for new procedures regarding meals and recreational activities in quarters for the members in his company. After considering various alternatives proposed by his lieutenants, the captain decides what the new procedures will be and informs the members of them on their next tours of duty.
The captain's actions in instituting these new procedures are
   A. *appropriate*, chiefly because he has shown the members that he is capable of decisive action
   B. *inappropriate*, chiefly because he should have given the members an opportunity to participate in the decision-making process
   C. *appropriate*, chiefly because he has clearly established his authority over matters occurring in quarters
   D. *inappropriate*, chiefly because he should have delegated the decision-making authority to one of his lieutenants

2. ___

3. An engine company captain, considering a change in the layout of hose in the hose bed, formulates a plan and discusses it briefly with each of his lieutenants on the change of tours. The lieutenants readily agree with the proposal, but the captain tells each one to think about the plan and discuss it with him in the near future.
Such action by the captain is generally
   A. *advisable*, chiefly because it may lead to consideration of alternatives to the captain's plan
   B. *not advisable*, chiefly because the captain should implement the plan he has already considered

3. ___

C. *advisable*, chiefly because the captain will have a basis for evaluating the contributions of his lieutenants
D. *not advisable*, chiefly because it shows indecision on the captain's part

4. A fire captain overhears a lieutenant explaining a certain evolution to a fireman. The captain knows that the procedure is about to be changed. Of the following, it would be MOST advisable for the captain to
   A. ignore the conversation and wait until everyone is formally notified of the new evolution
   B. step in and explain to the lieutenant and the fireman that instructions on the new evolution will be issued shortly
   C. take the lieutenant aside and tell him that the evolution will soon be changed
   D. wait until the lieutenant concludes his explanation, tell him about the new evolution, and ask him not to divulge the information until it is promulgated officially

4.___

5. Because of new guidelines that have been drawn up by the higher echelons of the department, a captain must introduce a number of changes which are expected to affect the work of the lieutenants and firemen under his command.
   Of the following, probably the BEST method of instituting a change in the operations of his organization is to
   A. introduce the change rapidly so as to forestall any resistance by the individuals affected
   B. introduce the change slowly enough so that the individuals affected will not feel the impact of the change
   C. show the individuals affected how the changes are related to past practices and objectives
   D. indicate that the changes are only tentative so that there will be no need for participation by the individuals affected in making decisions necessary to implement the change

5.___

6. A captain who had been transferred finds that the housekeeping in his new engine company is below standard. Although he concludes that changes in both committee work assignments and activities would improve matters, he feels that the firemen will resist any attempts at change.
   Of the following guidelines, which would probably be MOST effective in overcoming the resistance expected from the members?
   A. Announce the changes and threaten to discipline firemen who do not comply with the new procedures and standards
   B. Tell the members that the previous company commander was lax in enforcing standards and that changes would now be instituted

6.___

C. Introduce the changes on a tentative basis before making them permanent
D. Present the problem to the firemen as a group and invite their suggestions for possible changes

7. A captain instructing a fireman on the proper use of a Halligan tool asks the fireman to repeat the instructions in his own words.
The captain's approach is a
   A. *good* idea, chiefly because it will find out whether the member has been paying attention
   B. *poor* idea, chiefly because the member might be embarrassed
   C. *good* idea, chiefly because it will reveal whether the member understood the instructions
   D. *poor* idea, chiefly because repetition tends to waste time which could be used for additional training

7.___

8. The MOST acceptable of the following statements concerning the *grapevine* as a means of communication in an organization is that generally the *grapevine*
   A. can be depended upon as an accurate source of information
   B. should be used by officers to give work methods information quickly to the men
   C. is preferred by employees to regular channels as a means of receiving information
   D. flourishes most where good communications are lacking

8.___

9. The *grapevine* often appears as an informal channel of communication within units.
A company commander should MOST appropriately
   A. ignore it, chiefly because it will distort accurate information with unfounded rumors
   B. try to feed it accurate information, chiefly because it can be effective for quick communication
   C. try to suppress it, chiefly because it constitutes a threat to his authority
   D. try to limit its functioning to a few key issues, chiefly because it does not transmit confidential information effectively

9.___

10. A captain is asked by his battalion commander to evaluate the morale in his company. In making this evaluation, the captain decides that he must set up a criterion to measure the level of morale.
Of the following, probably the MOST appropriate criterion he can use is
   A. how the members get along with each other and with their officers
   B. the consistent ability of the company to produce results over prolonged periods of time and in a variety of assignments

10.___

C. the degree to which the members conform to the rules
and regulations and avoid making mistakes
D. the degree of complacency among the members in their
attitudes toward each other and toward the organization as a whole

11. Some company commanders make it a point to speak regularly
with their subordinates in order to find out what they
want to know, are interested in, and are receptive to.
This practice is generally
A. *undesirable*, chiefly because these commanders might
learn about unsubstantiated rumors which are better
ignored
B. *desirable*, chiefly because upward communication is
facilitated when higher-ranking officers make it a
practice to listen to their subordinates
C. *undesirable*, chiefly because listening to subordinates
rarely reveals their true feelings or the motivation
behind what they are trying to communicate
D. *desirable*, chiefly because upward communication normally produces fewer misunderstandings than downward
communication

11.___

12. Assume that, in order to motivate his subordinates and
promote efficiency in his command, a captain uses a strong
no nonsense approach and deliberately puts pressure on
his men to achieve goals much higher than he can reasonably
expect them to meet.
Of the following, the MOST likely result of the captain's
approach is that the men will
A. concentrate heavily on long-range tasks at the expense of those more immediately at hand
B. become frustrated and be motivated to band together
to beat the system
C. begin to set for themselves and achieve even higher
goals than those set by the captain
D. perform their firefighting tasks more effectively
than routine housekeeping or maintenance work

12.___

13. A fireman troubled by family problems tells you, his
captain, his personal problems make it difficult for him
to concentrate on his work or to sleep at night.
Of the following, generally the MOST helpful way for you
to handle this matter is to
A. listen to what he has to say and suggest that he seek
professional assistance
B. find out what the family problems are so that you may
advise him on how to rid himself of his troubles
C. relate similar experiences of your own to show that
his problem is not an uncommon one
D. advise him to forget his troubles and to concentrate
on more pleasant things

13.___

14. Assume that a fireman complains to you, his captain, that   14.___
    the lieutenant he works with most often has given him no
    recognition for the many times he has risked his life
    when fighting fires. Furthermore, the fireman claims that,
    because of his bravery, many lives were saved.
    Of the following, the BEST way to handle the fireman's
    complaint is to
        A. try to talk the fireman out of his complaint
        B. recommend a commendation for the fireman immediately
        C. check into the legitimacy of the fireman's complaint
        D. assure the fireman that you will transfer him to your
           group and observe his work more closely

15. During his first few months with a new company, a recently   15.___
    appointed captain pays particular attention to discovering
    the personal characteristics of his men and the way they
    are likely to respond to his leadership. As a result, he
    draws the following conclusions:
        I. The cooperative type of fireman who knows his job
           responds best to a democratic or *free-reign* kind of
           leadership
       II. The aggressive, hostile type of fireman responds best
           to autocratic leadership
      III. The insecure type of fireman responds best to demo-
           cratic or *free-reign* leadership
       IV. The individualist who knows his job responds best to
           autocratic leadership
    Which of the following choices includes ALL of the cap-
    tain's conclusions listed above that are generally CORRECT?
        A. I, II   B. I, III   C. II, IV   D. III, IV

16. When a newly-appointed fireman asks his commanding officer   16.___
    what would happen to the pump at a fire if the discharge
    gates of a working centrifugal pump were suddenly shut,
    the officer suggests that the fireman watch the men at the
    next fire and ask questions afterward if he still does not
    understand what governs the functioning of the pump under
    the circumstances mentioned.
    From the information supplied above, the MOST pertinent
    evaluation of this officer's conduct would be that he
        A. avoided his responsibility to train and orient new
           personnel under his command
        B. wanted the new member to get a lasting impression of
           the effect of a sudden closing of the discharge gates
        C. was certain the new member would be able to observe
           the results under fire conditions, without the need
           for further questions
        D. was practicing good leadership by anticipating an
           incident in which more experienced firefighters might
           play a role in the development of a new member

17. Sensing an element of hostility toward his company among
    residents of the low-income neighborhood in which his
    fire department unit is located, a company commander
    decides he must try to counteract the deleterious effect
    on morale and efficiency this antagonism is producing.
    He discusses the problem with his lieutenants and asks
    them to think about possible remedies. Then he arranges
    similar meetings with the men under his command and asks
    them also for suggestions. As a result of these discus-
    sions, a program for concerted action is devised and
    mutually agreed upon.
    Of the following conclusions which might be reached con-
    cerning the actions of this commanding officer, the MOST
    reasonable is that he
       A. resorted to extremely unorthodox methods in attempt-
          ing to solve a routine problem
       B. risked losing the respect of his men and fellow offi-
          cers
       C. did little or nothing himself (toward solving the
          problem)
       D. conducted himself in a manner which will probably
          enhance his reputation as a leader

                                                              17.____

18. A captain experiencing difficulty in dealing with a
    problem and coming to a specific decision on how to
    resolve it would probably be disturbed MOST by the fact
    that the
       A. necessity of making a decision must be considered
       B. pros and cons of possible alternatives must be
          compared
       C. potential risks and benefits must be evaluated
       D. decision may not prove to be a pleasant or popular
          one

                                                              18.____

19. A company commander would be likely to find a committee
    of members MOST useful when the
       A. data needed to solve problems are not readily avail-
          able
       B. authority of the committee to make decisions is clear-
          ly defined
       C. topics on the committee agenda are of minor impor-
          tance
       D. matters requiring decisions are beyond the authority
          of the individual committee members

                                                              19.____

20. Assume that in making a decision on an important matter
    affecting his command, a captain believes that there is
    only one way of handling the problem.
    In general, it is MOST likely that a decision based on
    such a belief would tend to be a
       A. *poor* one, mainly because the captain has probably not
          considered alternative solutions
       B. *good* one, mainly because such firm decision-making
          enhances the captain's ability to assert his authority

                                                              20.____

C. *poor* one, mainly because the captain's need to *play it safe* may prevent his making a rational decision
D. *good* one, mainly because it is not unusual to find only one alternative to the solution of a problem

———

KEY (CORRECT ANSWERS)

1. C
2. B
3. A
4. A
5. C

6. D
7. C
8. D
9. B
10. B

11. B
12. B
13. A
14. C
15. A

16. A
17. D
18. D
19. B
20. A

———

TEST 2

DIRECTIONS: Each question or incomplete statement is followed by several suggested answers or completions. Select the one that BEST answers the question or completes the statement. *PRINT THE LETTER OF THE CORRECT ANSWER IN THE SPACE AT THE RIGHT.*

1. A company commander takes a strongly authoritarian approach in dealing with his men.
   Of the following, the MOST likely result of this approach is
   A. slower compliance with orders because of increased feedback
   B. increased conformity by members to rules and regulations
   C. change in members' attitudes in the direction desired by the captain
   D. greater complexity of the command process

1.___

2. A captain, preparing recommendations for a training course to develop leadership qualities among newly-appointed lieutenants, lists the following elements as essential to effective leadership.
   Leadership
   I. depends as much on the group as it does on the leader
   II. requires conformity and acquiescence by the group
   III. depends on the group's commitment to the task at hand
   IV. depends on the interaction between the leader and those led

   The CORRECT answer is:
   A. I, III, IV
   C. I, II, III
   B. II, III, IV
   D. I, II, IV

2.___

3. You have decided, as company commander, to assign each of your lieutenants the authority and responsibility for maintaining company files for personnel matters, building inspections, and training. Each lieutenant will have prime responsibility for one of these areas.
   Delegation of this kind is generally
   A. *advisable*, chiefly because you will have greater opportunity to spot difficulties in each area more quickly
   B. *not advisable*, chiefly because each lieutenant will still depend on you for guidance
   C. *advisable*, chiefly because it will minimize the amount of responsibility you will have to retain over these functions
   D. *not advisable*, chiefly because such delegation of authority, once made, cannot be reclaimed without great difficulty

3.___

4. The one of the following which is likely to have the   4.___
GREATEST influence in making a company commander an effective manager is the ability to
    A. recognize his own weaknesses and minimize them
    B. emphasize the work process over the end product
    C. make a large number of decisions quickly and easily
    D. concentrate his efforts on the highest priorities

5. To promote efficiency and effectiveness in accordance with   5.___
current developments in the area of managerial process,
the fire department has introduced a management by objectives (MBO) program. The officers responsible for conducting this program have been evaluating it in terms of
potential impact on the operations of the department.
Some of the major benefits and weaknesses of managing by
objectives which they are studying are expressed in the
following four statements:
MBO
    I. forces clarification of organizational roles and
      structures
   II. tends to overemphasize qualitative factors at the
      expense of quantitative goals
 III. elicits commitment for performance
  IV. tends to emphasize long-range goals at the expense
      of short-range goals
According to the latest thinking about the advantages and
disadvantages of the MBO technique, which of the state-
ments given above should be accepted as CORRECT?
    A. I, II, III   B. II, III, IV
    C. I, III   D. II, IV

6. In discussing a memorandum covering two related subjects,   6.___
one of which will benefit his men slightly and the other
of which is expected to inconvenience them somewhat, a
company commander should be aware that the members are
MOST likely to
    A. pay more attention to the section that will benefit
      them than to the section that may inconvenience them
    B. pay more attention to the section that may incon-
      venience them than to the section that will benefit
      them
    C. pay equal attention to both sections
    D. largely ignore both sections

7. Assume that as captain you decide to meet with the firemen   7.___
in your company to discuss ways of improving community
relations with the neighborhood.
Of the following approaches you might take in holding this
group discussion, the one likely to be MOST productive is:
    A. Letting the group aim for broad, general goals rather
      than specific, detailed objectives
    B. Asking open-ended questions rather than those calling
      for *yes* or *no* answers

       C. Proceeding without a preplanned agenda in order to avoid restricting the discussion

       D. Participating in a taut, formal atmosphere rather than a casual, informal one

8. At a company drill, you as a captain cannot get the members to discuss their feelings on a new department policy. You decide to use the *buzz group* technique.
Of the following statements concerning the advantages of this technique, it is LEAST appropriate to state that it
       A. gives the men a chance to express their feelings without being directly identified
       B. gives the men a chance to see how others react to their suggestions
       C. permits the officer to avoid introducing an unpopular policy
       D. is good for getting the discussion going on non-controversial matters

  8.___

9. A newly-appointed captain confers with each of his lieutenants, all of whom have been in the company for more than 10 years. They tell the captain that the previous company commander had let them *run the company* while they were on duty and use their own discretion as to fire prevention inspections, drill subjects, etc. Since everything has worked out well thus far, the captain decides to go along with the policy of his predecessor.
This decision is
       A. *wise*, chiefly because it will assure his popularity with his subordinates
       B. *unwise*, chiefly because a captain should have a long-range plan of operations to carry out department policy
       C. *wise*, chiefly because his experienced lieutenants have informed him that this policy had worked successfully in the past
       D. *unwise*, chiefly because he should not have consulted with his subordinates before establishing his own policy

  9.___

10. As a captain, while you are on apparatus field inspection duty, one of your members reports that he has issued an order to a building owner to remedy a violation *forthwith*. The member states that the owner seems agitated and hostile and refuses to correct the condition. You decide to speak to the owner yourself.
In discussing this situation with the owner, it is MOST advisable for you to
       A. inform the owner firmly but bluntly that he is incorrect in insisting the condition does not require correction
       B. try to convince the owner that you are an expert in this area and that your knowledge should not be questioned

  10.___

C. express an appropriate degree of anger at the owner's refusal to correct an unsafe condition
D. stick to discussion of the specific violation, and avoid trying to convince the owner of the importance of correcting all fire hazards

11. Which of the following would generally be the BEST method for a captain to use in conducting drills in quarters in the use of a new power saw?

11.___

   A. Give informal oral instructions to two or three members at a time, followed by a review of the manufacturer's operating manual
   B. Conduct formal lectures combined with a written procedure summarizing the operating procedures
   C. Demonstrate the power saw and conduct informal group discussion on its use, making reference to the manufacturer's manual
   D. Allow each member to practice using the power saw after instructing them in its operation according to the manufacturer's manual

12. Assume that you are a captain who has under his command a lieutenant who is conscientious and otherwise capable, but who has trouble maintaining discipline because he lacks assertiveness. When he meets with you during changes of tours, he spends a good deal of time discussing the unruly behavior of his men, but does not seem to realize that the situation may result from his own deficiency.
For you to attempt to help the lieutenant understand that he may be largely at fault in this matter is

12.___

   A. *advisable*, mainly because the lieutenant's recognition of his own personality problems would relieve you of responsibility for giving him further guidance
   B. *inadvisable*, mainly because the lieutenant would become discouraged and even more insecure in his supervisory role
   C. *advisable*, mainly because recognition of his own poor practices would be a critical first step in enabling the lieutenant to overcome this problem
   D. *inadvisable*, mainly because personality improvement is a sensitive area necessitating referral to a trained professional

13. Assume that you a captain have talked repeatedly to a fireman about observing certain fire safety precautions which he has been neglecting but you have been unable to modify his habits. Annoyed by his indifferent attitude, you become concerned about losing your patience.
In dealing with this situation, generally the BEST of the following courses of action for you to take would be to

13.___

   A. hide your annoyance and keep talking to the fireman
   B. let the fireman know you are annoyed and be more severe with him

C. refer the fireman to one of your lieutenants who may be better able to talk to him

D. recommend that the fireman be transferred to another company

14. Assume that the performance of a lieutenant in your command has slipped noticeably over a period of several months from a level of high proficiency to a level of low proficiency. As you take measures to improve the lieutenant's performance, it would generally be
   A. *inadvisable* to explain to him exactly what is expected of him
   B. *advisable* to tell him that he is doing better work than he actually is
   C. *inadvisable* to tell him that he is not doing as good work as he should be
   D. *advisable* to praise him for the things that he has done well

14.___

15. In directing the actions of their subordinates, fire officers have well-defined expectations with respect to performance. Similarly, firemen who receive this direction have expectations regarding the qualifications of their officers. Following are three statements that might describe the expectations of subordinates:
   I. An officer must be technically skilled in his work even if he rarely practices his skill on the job
   II. Symbols of office and titles of authority have to do with the willingness of subordinates to follow orders given by an officer
   III. To gain respect, an officer who holds a particular rank should have what his subordinates consider the appropriate background for that rank

The CORRECT answer is:
   A. I, III   B. I, II   C. II, III   D. I, II, III

15.___

16. In general, the one of the following conditions under which a fire officer is MOST likely to accept increased responsibility is when he is
   A. fearful of failure in carrying out his regular tasks
   B. resigned to being left indefinitely in his present job unless he accepts increased responsibility
   C. fairly secure in his job
   D. authoritarian in his basic attitudes

16.___

17. Assume that you are a company commander and one of your lieutenants reports that a fireman who recently came into your company after three years of service with another unit is performing his duties in a slipshod, indifferent manner. The officer describes the member as antagonistic and resentful of suggestions for improving his work. The lieutenant asks you to take action or suggest a course of action to remedy the situation.

17.___

Of the following, the MOST appropriate step for you to
take would generally be to
  A. assign the fireman to your own working group so that
     you may be able to observe him more closely
  B. ask the informal leaders among members in the company
     to bring pressure on the fireman to get into line
  C. suggest that the lieutenant write down instances of
     the fireman's poor performance preparatory to filing
     of charges
  D. cite the fireman during company drills as an example
     of unacceptable attitude and performance

18. A company commander frequently works alongside his men on   18.___
    maintenance chores in quarters in order to set a good
    example for them.
    The practice followed by this officer is generally
      A. *recommended*, chiefly because setting an example should
         improve the performance of the men
      B. *not recommended*, chiefly because his men may fail to
         follow orders during fire and emergency situations
      C. *recommended*, chiefly because it may enable him to
         develop good personal contacts and improved relation-
         ships with his men
      D. *not recommended*, chiefly because his men may feel
         that he lacks confidence in their ability to do the
         job on their own

19. The captain of a ladder company begins a post-fire   19.___
    critique by finding fault with the performance of the
    roof man and the irons man in comparison with the work
    of other members who had these assignments.
    The method used by this captain is generally
      A. *appropriate*, chiefly because the fireman being criti-
         cized will tend to acknowledge and accept responsi-
         bility for the mistakes
      B. *inappropriate*, chiefly because discussion of past
         errors has little learning value for future incidents
      C. *appropriate*, chiefly because it forms cohesive group
         attitudes and improves good team relationships
      D. *inappropriate*, chiefly because public ventilation of
         personal shortcomings is not likely to produce
         constructive results

20. In conducting a counseling interview with a fireman, which   20.___
    of the following guidelines is it generally MOST appro-
    priate for a fire captain to follow?
      A. Use non-directive techniques to encourage the fireman
         to talk freely and think the problem through himself
      B. Focus discussion and avoid wasting time by asking
         direct questions that can be answered with *yes* or *no*
         responses
      C. Use the reflective summary approach to indicate
         approval of the positive behaviors exhibited by the
         fireman

D. Place the fireman at ease by discussing some unrelated topic at length if the subject of the interview is an especially unpleasant one

—

KEY (CORRECT ANSWERS)

1.	B	11.	D
2.	A	12.	C
3.	A	13.	B
4.	D	14.	D
5.	C	15.	A
6.	A	16.	C
7.	B	17.	A
8.	C	18.	D
9.	B	19.	D
10.	D	20.	A

—

EXAMINATION SECTION
TEST 1

DIRECTIONS: Each question or incomplete statement is followed by several suggested answers or completions. Select the one that BEST answers the question or completes the statement. *PRINT THE LETTER OF THE CORRECT ANSWER IN THE SPACE AT THE RIGHT.*

1. When positive methods fail to achieve conformity with accepted standards of conduct or performance, a negative type of action, punitive in nature, usually must follow. The one of the following that is usually considered LEAST important for the success of such punishment or negative discipline is that it be
   A. certain   B. swift   C. severe   D. consistent   1.___

2. The principle relating to the number of subordinates who can be supervised effectively by one supervisor is COMMONLY known as   2.___
   A. span of control
   B. delegation of authority
   C. optimum personnel assignment
   D. organizational factor

3. The one of the following administrative functions for which a committee is LEAST useful is   3.___
   A. collecting and distributing information about changes in techniques of fire investigation
   B. relieving fire marshals of their routine assignments so that they may respond to multiple-alarm fire scenes
   C. resolving conflicts between competing interest groups within the division of fire investigation
   D. planning stakeouts involving several groups of marshals

4. Which of the following statements concerning the delegation of work to subordinate employees is generally CORRECT?   4.___
   A. A supervisor's personal attitude toward delegation has a minimal effect on his skill in delegating.
   B. A willingness to let subordinates make mistakes has a place in work delegation.
   C. The element of trust has little impact on the effectiveness of work delegation.
   D. The establishment of controls does not enhance the process of delegation.

5. Of the following, the MAIN advantage for a supervisor in relying upon oral rather than written communication to keep his subordinates informed is that oral communication   5.___
   A. facilitates speedy interchange between the supervisor and his subordinates
   B. reinforces the supervisor's control over the actions of his subordinates

    C. eliminates misunderstandings and rumors
    D. enables the supervisor to maintain a broad span of
       control

6. The one of the following which BEST describes the rate at   6.___
which a trainee learns departmental procedures is that
he PROBABLY will learn
    A. at a constant rate if the material to be learned is
       complex
    B. slowly in the beginning and then faster as training
       continues
    C. at a constant rate if the material to be learned is
       lengthy
    D. quickly at first, then more slowly for a while

7. Don't ask one employee to work for two supervisors.   7.___
Of the following, the BEST justification for this statement is that the
    A. *employee* may become confused as to work priorities
    B. *employee* may consolidate incompatible work operations
    C. *supervisors* may assign him insignificant tasks
    D. *supervisors* may fail to delegate the necessary
       authority to him

8. Departmental policies are usually broad rules or guides   8.___
for action. It is important for a supervisor to understand his role with respect to policy implementation.
Of the following, the MOST accurate description of this
role is that a supervisor should
    A. be apologetic toward his subordinates when applying
       unpopular policies to them
    B. act within policy limits, although he can attempt to
       influence policy change by making his thoughts and
       observations known to his superior
    C. arrange his activities so that he is able to deal
       simultaneously with situations that involve several
       policy matters
    D. refrain as much as possible from exercising permis-
       sible discretion in applying policy to matters under
       his control

9. Of the following, the PRIMARY responsibility of a super-   9.___
visor is to
    A. lead and train his subordinates to perform their
       duties
    B. evaluate ideas for improving work methods
    C. establish working relations with other supervisors
    D. achieve high morale among his employees

10. The practice of a supervisor in instructing the members   10.___
of his group to report directly to him and to take their
orders directly from him is GENERALLY
    A. *good*, chiefly because it maintains unity of command
    B. *poor*, chiefly because other supervisors will not be
       aware of the supervisor's activities or whereabouts

C. *good*, chiefly because large organizations run more efficiently if each person talks or works with only one individual

D. *poor*, chiefly because a member who is accustomed to taking orders from one individual will not adjust well if transferred to another group

11. Of the following, the MOST effective way to teach a large group a specific manipulative operation on a new piece of photographic equipment is to
   A. let the trainees instruct themselves by working through a carefully sequenced and pretested series of steps leading to mastery of the operation
   B. demonstrate the operation, let the trainees practice it, and then criticize their performance until it is mastered
   C. provide the trainees with a manual describing the operation and a set of carefully supervised written exercises for practicing the skills implicit in the operation
   D. lecture the trainees on how to perform the operation and then have them discuss it as a group

11.___

12. Assume that you are a supervisor and that Smith, one of the men in your unit, informs you that another, Jones, has been creating antagonism and friction within the unit by dealing in an unnecessarily gruff manner with his co-workers. Smith's remarks confirm your own observations.
   In handling this situation, the MOST effective procedure you could follow would PROBABLY be to
   A. ask Smith to act as an informal counselor to Jones and report the results to you
   B. counsel the other employees in your unit on methods of changing the attitudes of people
   C. interview Jones and help him to understand his problem
   D. order Jones to carry out his responsibilities with greater consideration for the feelings of his co-workers

12.___

13. You have been assigned to supervise the planning of a program of arson prevention, designed to deter arsonists and to acquaint the public with the problem. As part of this program, employees will participate in lectures, meetings, and discussions with civic and community groups. In laying out the content of the program, you should reinforce its positive aspects by including provision for the employees to
   A. instruct the general public on methods of fire-setting and use of incendiary devices
   B. point out the difficulties involved in detecting and investigating arson
   C. emphasize the problems involved in obtaining arson convictions
   D. stress the economic impact of arson on every citizen

13.___

14. Assume that a supervisor has a highly critical and nega-   14.___
tive attitude toward the men under his supervision. The
MOST likely consequence of such an attitude will be that
the men will
    A. develop an unhealthy reliance on his direction
    B. take more initiative in making decisions
    C. become dissatisfied with their work
    D. disregard him and establish their own work goals

15. Of the following, the MOST effective method of improving   15.___
communications between a supervisor and the employees
under his supervision is for him to
    A. use direct, simple language in dealing with them
    B. reinforce his words with action
    C. utilize and encourage feedback from his subordinates
    D. make sure that his communications include enough
       repetition to enforce the message

16. Ascertaining and improving the level of morale in a   16.___
public agency is one of the responsibilities of a conscientious supervisor.
The one of the following aspects of subordinates' behavior
which is NOT an indication of low morale is
    A. lower-level employees participating in organizational
       decision-making
    B. careless treatment of equipment
    C. general deterioration of personal appearance
    D. formation of cliques

17. The one of the following which is the MAIN disadvantage   17.___
of assigning employees into specialized groups on the
basis of work tasks is that job specialization may
    A. foster destructive competition and friction within
       the organization
    B. increase both the cost and the amount of time
       required to train employees
    C. complicate the problem of developing job controls
    D. result in unnecessary duplication of equipment

18. A supervisor should be aware that MOST subordinates will   18.___
ask questions at meetings or group discussions in order to
    A. stimulate other employees to express their opinions
    B. discover how they may be affected by the subjects
       under discussion
    C. display their knowledge of the topics under discussion
    D. consume time in order to avoid returning to their
       normal tasks

19. Employees may resist changes in agency operations even   19.___
though such changes are often necessary. If you, as a
supervisor, are attempting to introduce a necessary
change in your unit, the first thing you should do is
explain the reasons for it to your staff.
Your NEXT step should be to

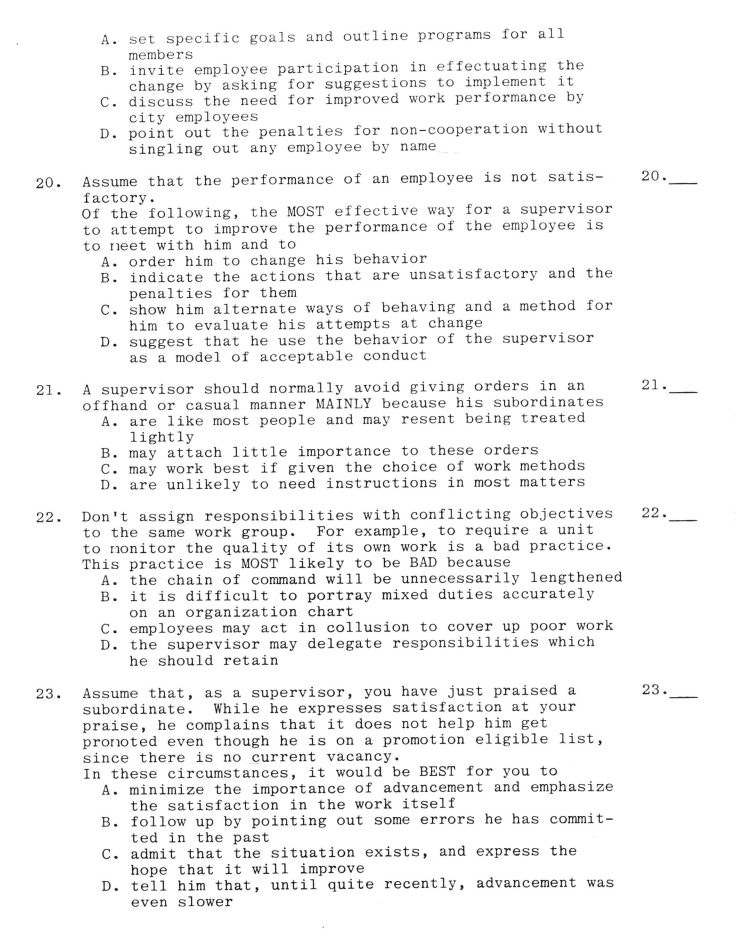

     A. set specific goals and outline programs for all
       members
     B. invite employee participation in effectuating the
       change by asking for suggestions to implement it
     C. discuss the need for improved work performance by
       city employees
     D. point out the penalties for non-cooperation without
       singling out any employee by name

20. Assume that the performance of an employee is not satis-   20.___
    factory.
    Of the following, the MOST effective way for a supervisor
    to attempt to improve the performance of the employee is
    to meet with him and to
     A. order him to change his behavior
     B. indicate the actions that are unsatisfactory and the
       penalties for them
     C. show him alternate ways of behaving and a method for
       him to evaluate his attempts at change
     D. suggest that he use the behavior of the supervisor
       as a model of acceptable conduct

21. A supervisor should normally avoid giving orders in an   21.___
    offhand or casual manner MAINLY because his subordinates
     A. are like most people and may resent being treated
       lightly
     B. may attach little importance to these orders
     C. may work best if given the choice of work methods
     D. are unlikely to need instructions in most matters

22. Don't assign responsibilities with conflicting objectives   22.___
    to the same work group. For example, to require a unit
    to monitor the quality of its own work is a bad practice.
    This practice is MOST likely to be BAD because
     A. the chain of command will be unnecessarily lengthened
     B. it is difficult to portray mixed duties accurately
       on an organization chart
     C. employees may act in collusion to cover up poor work
     D. the supervisor may delegate responsibilities which
       he should retain

23. Assume that, as a supervisor, you have just praised a   23.___
    subordinate. While he expresses satisfaction at your
    praise, he complains that it does not help him get
    promoted even though he is on a promotion eligible list,
    since there is no current vacancy.
    In these circumstances, it would be BEST for you to
     A. minimize the importance of advancement and emphasize
       the satisfaction in the work itself
     B. follow up by pointing out some errors he has commit-
       ted in the past
     C. admit that the situation exists, and express the
       hope that it will improve
     D. tell him that, until quite recently, advancement was
       even slower

24. Assume that a supervisor gives his subordinate instruc- 24.___
tions which are appropriate and clear, but the subordi-
nate refuses to follow them.
Of the following, it would be MOST appropriate for the
supervisor to
   A. try to find out what the employee objects to
   B. take disciplinary action immediately
   C. remind the subordinate about supervisory authority
      and threaten him with discipline
   D. insist that the subordinate carry out the order
      promptly

25. In preparing a letter or a report, a supervisor may wish 25.___
to persuade the recipient of the desirability of some
idea or course of action.
The BEST way to accomplish this would be for the super-
visor to
   A. encourage the recipient to react promptly to the
      suggestion
   B. express each aspect of the suggestion in a separate
      paragraph
   C. present the subject matter in the first paragraph
   D. point out the potential benefits for the recipient

KEY (CORRECT ANSWERS)

1. C		11. B	
2. A		12. C	
3. B		13. D	
4. B		14. C	
5. A		15. C	
6. D		16. A	
7. A		17. A	
8. B		18. B	
9. A		19. B	
10. A		20. C	

21. B
22. C
23. C
24. A
25. D

TEST 2

DIRECTIONS: Each question or incomplete statement is followed by several suggested answers or completions. Select the one that BEST answers the question or completes the statement. *PRINT THE LETTER OF THE CORRECT ANSWER IN THE SPACE AT THE RIGHT.*

1. Leadership has been defined as the art of inducing subor-   1.___
   dinates to accomplish their assignments with zeal and
   confidence.
   Following are three statements concerning leadership that
   MIGHT be correct.
   - I. Leadership depends primarily on the personal traits
     of the leader and is minimally affected by the situ-
     ation from which the leader emerges and in which he
     operates.
   - II. A leader should be both part of a group and distinct
     from it.
   - III. A leader will choose the most effective means for
     him to achieve enterprise objectives, irrespective
     of whether the means are permissive, authoritarian,
     or in between.
   Which of the following choices lists all of the above
   statements that are generally CORRECT?
   A. I and II, but not III   B. I and III, but not II
   C. II and III, but not I   D. I, II, and III

2. A certain officer assumes that his subordinates understand   2.___
   and attach the same importance to situations in the work
   environment that he does.
   This assumption by the officer is generally
   A. *correct*, primarily because people are basically
      objective and are able to agree on important matters
   B. *incorrect*, primarily because people tend to over-
      react to mildly unpleasant situations and to exag-
      gerate their importance
   C. *correct*, primarily because people are usually able
      to see pleasant and unpleasant things with equal
      accuracy
   D. *incorrect*, primarily because people behave on the
      basis of the perceived world, and their perceptions
      are to a large extent determined by their needs

3. Morale includes the employees' attitude toward the depart-   3.___
   ment as a whole.
   As far as the relationship between productivity and
   morale is concerned, MOST recent studies indicate that
   A. high morale results in high productivity while low
      morale does not result in low productivity
   B. low morale results in low productivity while high
      morale does not result in high productivity
   C. morale and productivity are not significantly related
   D. as morale increases, productivity also increases

4. Departmentation is the process of grouping various activi-   4.___
   ties into separate units. One method of doing this is to
   group activities in accordance with the functions of the
   enterprise.
   Which of the following would generally NOT be considered
   an advantage of grouping activities on the basis of func-
   tion?
   It
   A. facilitates specialization by grouping together func-
      tions that belong together
   B. gives high-level officials an opportunity to learn
      the entire range of different functions
   C. simplifies coordination since each unit performs one
      type of activity
   D. makes the outstanding abilities of the highest-level
      officials available to the entire enterprise

5. Which of the following is LEAST likely to result from   5.___
   greater decentralization of the fire department?
   A. Relieving higher authorities of responsibilities
   B. Improving morale at the local level
   C. Developing leadership ability among subordinates
   D. Providing more time for planning to high-ranking
      officials

6. In addition to the formal structure in an organization,   6.___
   an informal organization often develops which includes
   all the relations and interrelations of people in the
   hierarchy who work together.
   Which of the following statements concerning informal
   organizations is LEAST likely to be correct?
   A. People band into formal groups which usually corres-
      pond to hierarchical groupings.
   B. An informal status system assigns roles to indivi-
      duals.
   C. An underground communication system develops which
      is often rapid and subtle.
   D. Informal groups govern the behavior of people to
      an extent that sometimes interferes with formal
      supervision.

7. Following are four statements concerning delegation of   7.___
   authority by superior officers to subordinates that
   MIGHT be correct.
   I. Superior officers cannot escape, through delegation,
      responsibility for the activities of subordinates.
   II. Wherever possible, subordinates should be encouraged
      to delegate decisions upward in the organization
      structure.
   III. Once a subordinate accepts an assignment, his respon-
      sibility to his superior for performance is absolute.
   IV. Responsibility for actions cannot be greater than
      that implied by the authority delegated, nor should
      it be less.

Which of the following choices lists all of the above statements that are generally CORRECT?
- A. I and III, but not II and IV
- B. III and IV, but not I and II
- C. I, II, and III, but not IV
- D. I, III, and IV, but not II

8. Decentralization is a fundamental aspect of delegation; to the extent that authority is not delegated, it is centralized.
In general, the degree of decentralization of authority in a department
- A. *increases* as the number of operations affected by decisions at lower levels of the departmental hierarchy decreases
- B. *decreases* as the number of decisions made lower down the departmental hierarchy increases
- C. *increases* as the number of people to be consulted and their rank in the departmental hierarchy decreases
- D. *decreases* as the importance of decisions made at the lower levels of the departmental hierarchy increases

8.___

9. Our own characteristics affect the characteristics we are more likely to see in others.
Following are three statements concerning the way individuals perceive others that MIGHT be correct.
- I. A person with authoritarian tendencies is more sensitive to the psychological or personality characteristics of other people than is a non-authoritarian.
- II. The categories we use in describing other people are generally different from those we use in describing ourselves.
- III. For people we do not like, we perceive most accurately their traits that are unlike our own, and least accurately their traits that are similar to our own.
Which of the following choices lists all of the above statements that are generally CORRECT?
- A. II, but not I and III
- B. III, but not I and II
- C. I and III, but not II
- D. I, II, and III

9.___

10. Assume that a problem-solving team consists of a deputy chief, a battalion chief, and a lieutenant. All three are well-qualified to contribute to the solution of a certain problem.
If the order of problem-solving communication moves from the deputy chief to the battalion chief to the lieutenant, communication will generally be _____ adequate solution than if the order were the reverse.
- A. *more inhibited*, but with a more
- B. *less inhibited*, with a more
- C. *more inhibited*, with a less
- D. *less inhibited*, but with a less

10.___

11. In the fire department, a high degree of cooperation is   11.___
    required among members at all levels.
    Following are three statements on obtaining group accep-
    tance and cooperation that MIGHT be correct:
        I. A supervisor should try to demonstrate that his
           interests and the interests of the group are basically
           the same
       II. A strong leader can sometimes get a group to submerge
           some of its interests in order to achieve organiza-
           tional objectives
      III. A leader must recognize that men do not generally
           like to work together for a common purpose
    Which of the following choices lists all of the above
    statements that are generally CORRECT?
        A. I and II, but not III   B. I and III, but not II
        C. II and III, but not I   D. I, II, and III

12. An organization is an arrangement of people-to-people   12.___
    relationships in a formal setting. By following recom-
    mended principles, the organization should move forward
    smoothly toward achieving the goal. Unfortunately, due
    to a number of variables, the avenue of approach to the
    goal becomes difficult, obstructed, and deflected.
    Which of the following is MOST likely to be an aspect of
    the informal organization that impedes progress toward
    organizational goals?
        A. Lack of a scientific approach to planning
        B. Resistance to conformity by the people in the
           organization
        C. Unclear perception of the nature of the goals to
           be achieved
        D. Failure to assign responsibility and authority for
           decision-making

13. Whenever possible, a certain company commander, when   13.___
    giving orders to subordinates, explains the facts or
    conditions that have made the order necessary.
    This practice is generally
        A. *advisable*, chiefly because it will give members a
           sense of importance and responsibility regarding
           their work
        B. *inadvisable*, chiefly because members will tend to
           discuss the order rather than carry it out
        C. *advisable*, chiefly because each member will feel
           that the order applies only to him
        D. *inadvisable*, chiefly because it will convey the
           impression that the order is of an arbitrary nature

14. Assume that a subordinate comes to you, a company com-   14.___
    mander, and wishes to discuss a personal problem when
    you have the time.
    For you to agree to discuss the subordinate's personal
    problem would generally be

A. *advisable*, chiefly because you should demonstrate a sincere interest in your subordinates as individuals
B. *inadvisable*, chiefly because other members under your command may resent such special attention being given to this subordinate
C. *advisable*, chiefly because one of your major supervisory duties is to give advice to employees about their personal problems
D. *inadvisable*, chiefly because any involvement in the personal problems of subordinates may lead to favoritism in job assignments

15. A state commission has recently recommended a policy of decentralizing city agencies by granting greater decision-making powers to borough or community governments. Of the following, an exception to this policy in the fire department is MOST likely to be made in the area of
   A. fire prevention activities
   B. firefighting operations
   C. fire investigation
   D. community relations

15.___

16. A company commander is trying to implement an informal system of employee performance evaluation. As part of this system, he conducts periodic interviews with members of his command to review their job performance. During an interview, one member complains that the company commander is inaccurate and unfair in his criticisms of the member's performance. The member states that he wishes to discuss his work performance with the battalion chief.
Of the following, the MOST appropriate action for the company commander to take in this situation would be to
   A. tell the member to wait a few days and then decide whether he wants to see the battalion chief
   B. tell the member that since the evaluation procedure is informal, there is no need for him to speak to the battalion chief
   C. find other aspects of the member's performance to praise in order to try to dissuade him from speaking to the battalion chief
   D. tell the member that he should feel free to discuss the matter with the battalion chief

16.___

17. Assume that a company commander wishes to teach a new fireman a difficult task involving the use of equipment. The task consists of many steps, with the difficult parts of the task mixed in with the easy ones.
For the task to be performed properly, these steps should be done in the correct order.
In this situation, which of the following is generally the MOST advisable training procedure for the company commander to follow?
Teach the

17.___

    A. steps to the fireman by proceeding from the easiest to the most difficult
    B. task in sequence by letting the fireman perform the easier steps first and the company commander the more difficult ones
    C. fireman so that he completes each step in the sequence that should be followed in performing the task
    D. more difficult steps first so that the fireman can learn the less difficult steps more quickly

18. The CENTRAL idea underlying the concept of span of control is that
    A. a superior can only supervise a fixed number of subordinates
    B. every subordinate should have one and only one boss
    C. there are limits to the number of subordinates a superior can effectively supervise
    D. a superior should have as small a number of subordinates as possible

19. As a company commander, you are continually evaluating the performance of your subordinates.
Of the following, the MAJOR objective of such performance evaluation should be to
    A. serve as the basis for the assignment of duties to subordinates
    B. aid in the improvement of employee effectiveness
    C. provide data upon which to decide who is eligible for special privileges
    D. furnish standards against which the performance of all employees may be compared

20. Assume that a subordinate tells his company commander that he doesn't feel capable of performing certain duties as well as other members of the company and that he is considering requesting a transfer.
During such an interview, the one of the following approaches that would generally be MOST advisable for the company commander to take is to
    A. assure the subordinate that he is doing his job well
    B. encourage the subordinate to discuss the problem more fully
    C. suggest a program of training that will improve the subordinate's ability
    D. advise the subordinate that he need not worry as long as his performance is not criticized

21. Under certain circumstances, a captain may wish to reduce the number of orders he gives to subordinates.
Of the following, the MOST effective way to do this is for the captain to
    A. encourage subordinates to ask him questions
    B. issue instructions in a manner subordinates will consider appropriate

C. give all the orders required to perform a particular task at the same time

D. emphasize to his subordinates the importance of consultation among themselves

22. Assume that a captain is considering disciplinary action against a subordinate who has committed a minor offense. Which of the following factors should be considered LEAST important in determining the severity of the disciplinary action?
The

A. subordinate's prior record as a member of the department

B. presence of mitigating or aggravating circumstances

C. nature of the subordinate's misconduct

D. subordinate's popularity with other members of the unit

22.____

23. As authority flows downward from an organizational superior to a subordinate, responsibility is created by reason of such delegated authority.
Which of the following is MOST likely to flow upward in proportion to that responsibility?
A. Communication   B. Accountability
C. Control   D. Power

23.____

24. In many formal organizations, an informal relationship exists among its members that is referred to as the grapevine.
A company commander who wishes to keep his subordinates as fully informed as possible should generally consider the grapevine to be

A. *helpful*, primarily because it avoids the necessity of establishing formal lines of communication

B. *harmful*, primarily because it usually interferes with formal efforts to transmit information

C. *helpful*, primarily because it is a valuable part of the informal organization which can be effective for quick communication

D. *harmful*, primarily because superiors have no opportunity to feed accurate information into the grapevine

24.____

25. Orders and procedures are often written or announced with repetition and duplication in the way they are worded.
This practice is generally

A. *proper*, mainly because repetition helps subordinates understand better

B. *improper*, mainly because redundancy in expression is wasteful

C. *proper*, mainly because those who prepare orders and procedures need not be proficient in editorial skills

D. *improper*, mainly because subordinates should understand procedures without repetition

25.____

KEY (CORRECT ANSWERS)

1. C		11. A
2. D		12. B
3. C		13. A
4. B		14. A
5. A		15. B
6. A		16. D
7. D		17. B
8. C		18. C
9. B		19. B
10. C		20. B

21. A
22. D
23. B
24. C
25. A

EXAMINATION SECTION

TEST 1

DIRECTIONS: Each question or incomplete statement is followed by several suggested answers or completions. Select the one that BEST answers the question or completes the statement. *PRINT THE LETTER OF THE CORRECT ANSWER IN THE SPACE AT THE RIGHT.*

1. Of the following duties to be performed, an officer would be LEAST justified in delegating to a member, rather than performing personally, the
   A. inspection of committee work
   B. preparation of a report of an investigation of a complaint
   C. follow-up training of a recently transferred member
   D. making out of hydrant inspection cards

   1.___

2. Several times during a drill, an officer restates the major points of his lecture using different words. This teaching technique is MOST appropriate when
   A. one of the men in the group is slower than the rest
   B. the average man in the group finds the material difficult
   C. he himself is somewhat unclear about aspects of the subject matter
   D. the amount of material to be covered would not ordinarily fill the available time

   2.___

3. For a captain to permit his lieutenants to participate in the decision-making process is generally desirable, when practicable, primarily because
   A. it leads to the elimination of grievances
   B. better solutions may be obtained
   C. individual development requires an ever-expanding view of operations
   D. the captain is forced to *keep on his toes* under the stimulation of interchange of ideas

   3.___

4. When using a standardized survey report form, it generally is NOT advisable to make an inspection of the facilities in the strict sequence of the items on the form primarily because the
   A. sequence of the items in the form may not correspond to the physical arrangement of the occupancy or structure
   B. members performing inspection duty will be more likely to make errors of omission rather than commission on the forms
   C. occupancy or structure may require a multi-inspector, multi-page form inspectional approach
   D. procedure does not permit distribution of tasks among all members participating in the inspection

   4.___

5. While giving job instructions on a new tool, an officer   5.___
   is asked by a member why the operation was not performed
   in a different manner. The method suggested included some
   actions which could cause injury. The officer answered
   that the method he was demonstrating was the correct one,
   that the suggested method was unsafe, and that there was
   no point in discussing wrong methods. The officer's
   approach to the question was
       A. *proper*, mainly because the members will not have the
          chance to pick up bad habits
       B. *improper*, mainly because the officer did not consider
          the possibility of modifying the suggestion to make
          it safer
       C. *proper*, mainly because speed of learning is most
          rapid when only one method is followed
       D. *improper*, mainly because hazards of incorrect methods
          can be avoided if they are known

6. An officer is to hold a drill on a new operation which is   6.___
   long and complicated. The one of the following measures
   that is MOST important in planning for this drill is to
       A. reserve sufficient time for the drill so that it can
          be presented completely and unhurriedly
       B. schedule daily repetition of the drill until it is
          mastered by the group
       C. obtain the assistance of experienced members in
          demonstrating the operation and correcting the
          performance of members of the group
       D. break up the operation into small instructional units
          and cover one unit at a time

7. Of the following, the MAIN reason for a fire officer to   7.___
   stress safety is to
       A. develop a respect for danger in all members
       B. replace ignorance with practical knowledge leading
          to the elimination of unfounded fears
       C. establish a safety-conscious work atmosphere in which
          the men seek safer operating methods
       D. reduce the degree to which experienced members express
          impatience and contempt for *restrictive* safety
          practices

8. People are ingenious at preserving their points of view   8.___
   and maintaining their biases.
   This attitude is LEAST likely to apply to matters relating
   to
       A. grievances   B. personnel assignment
       C. job skills training   D. fire prevention education

9. A fire officer who, when making assignments, takes into   9.___
   consideration the emotional state of a man under severe
   strain is acting
       A. *improperly*, mainly because the other men will resent
          any signs of favoritism

   B. *properly*, mainly because in some situations the
      affected man may not be dependable
   C. *improperly*, mainly because each man is getting the
      same salary and should be expected to exert the same
      effort
   D. *properly*, mainly because the man will be a more highly
      motivated employee when his situation returns to
      normal

10. The outcome that is MOST likely to result from setting   10.___
    work standards slightly higher than subordinates can
    achieve with ease is that they will have
    A. clearly defined and perceivable objectives
    B. a desire to avoid potential failure
    C. the opportunity to enjoy gratifying success
    D. an area about which they can safely complain

11. A recently assigned officer is concerned about the fact   11.___
    that he has taken an instantaneous liking to some of his
    men whereas one just seems to antagonize him. Of the
    following, the MOST useful first step he could take with
    respect to this member is to
    A. determine the chances of transferring him out of the
       company
    B. tactfully ascertain from other officers their reac-
       tions to this man and his reputation as a fireman
    C. recognize that this is the well-known *halo* effect and
       make a conscious effort to be fair to this man
    D. explain his feelings to his chief and ask for his
       advice

12. Safety experts generally regard attempting to determine   12.___
    who is to blame when investigating accidents to be a
    A. *good* practice, mainly because a violation of safety
       rules should not go unpunished
    B. *poor* practice, mainly because an attitude of *covering
       up* makes it difficult to uncover the facts
    C. *good* practice, mainly because persons involved in
       accidents through no fault of their own want to be
       exonerated
    D. *poor* practice, mainly because the multitude of factors
       that *cause* accidents generally makes it difficult, if
       not impossible, to fix the blame

13. A company is faced with a troublesome local problem. The   13.___
    company commander calls all his officers to a meeting,
    outlines the problem, and asks them to give spontaneously
    any ideas that occur to them as possible ways of handling
    it. Each idea suggested is written down, and later dis-
    cussed carefully. The CHIEF advantage of the procedure
    employed by the company commander is that
    A. time is not wasted on needless talk
    B. ideas are obtained which otherwise might not be
       developed

    C. there is less tendency for the meeting to stray from
       the subject under discussion
    D. officers receive training in analysis of problems and
       evaluation of solutions

14. While taking up lines during freezing weather, a newly-   14.___
    appointed officer sees a veteran fireman freeing hose from
    ice by turning it back on itself and pulling it loose.
    Of the following, the BEST procedure for the officer to
    follow in this situation is to
    A. question the man to find out whether he knows a
       better and safer way to perform this work
    B. assign the man to other duties and assign another
       member to pick up the hose
    C. advise the member that if the hose is damaged he will
       be subject to charges for abusing department property
    D. order the man to get the necessary equipment to do
       the job properly

15. Before conducting a drill on a new tool, an officer   15.___
    prepared a detailed job breakdown and distributed copies
    to members of the company several days prior to the drill
    so that they could become familiar with it beforehand.
    The MAIN error in the officer's procedure was in
    A. distributing the job breakdown without approval of
       the Division of Training
    B. distributing the job breakdown before, rather than
       after, conducting the drill
    C. preparing the job breakdown before conducting the
       drill and ascertaining the points that cause diffi-
       culty
    D. using the job breakdown as an instruction sheet for
       the learners rather than a teaching tool for the
       instructor

16. When unexpected obstacles arise during the course of   16.___
    operations, the officer must find means of overcoming
    them. Of the following, the MOST important factor in
    this endeavor is the officer's
    A. attitude   B. advance planning
    C. training   D. knowledge of procedures

17. A new procedure is about to be instituted in your division. 17.___
    Before presenting it to your men, you try to think of what
    objections they may raise and how to deal with these ob-
    jections. Of the following, the BEST reason for this
    practice is that the
    A. men will respect your competence when you can handle
       their objections on the spot
    B. analysis involved will help you to better understand
       the new procedure
    C. objections can be channeled upwards and the procedure
       revised before it is implemented
    D. knowledge you have of your men's ways of thinking
       and behaving will be increased

18. A new chauffeur develops a tendency to overspeed the   18.____
    engine before upshifting gears. As his superior, the
    MOST effective measure for you to take would be to
       A. report the member's deficiency to the Division of
          Safety
       B. request that the man be relieved of his assignment
       C. institute corrective training emphasizing both theory
          and performance
       D. discuss this condition with the man to get at its
          cause

19. A company commander institutes a policy of minimizing   19.____
    the amount of information he passes on to his officers
    since he feels they are overburdened with details. This
    practice is
       A. *proper*; it is part of the company commander's job to
          act as a buffer for his men
       B. *improper*; the company commander is trying to carry
          too many responsibilities on his own shoulders
       C. *proper*; his leadership strength is increased by the
          degree to which his officers turn to him for guidance
       D. *improper*; the officers lack information which may be
          necessary to proper performance of their duties

20. A good leader encourages subordinates to use their ini-   20.____
    tiative but realizes that such a practice has a price.
    Of the following, the MAIN drawback is that subordinates
    will occasionally
       A. overstep the bounds of their authority
       B. make errors in judgment
       C. duplicate work of others
       D. engage in fruitless experimentation

21. It is proposed that the fire department adopt a uniform   21.____
    department-wide filing system consisting of numbered
    folders and an alphabetical index. Under this system,
    all reports and other communications of the department
    would be listed in an index and the numbered folder in
    which that subject should be filed would be indicated.
    Such a system would be
       A. *desirable*, mainly because personnel newly assigned
          to a unit would know where to look for information
       B. *undesirable*, mainly because the needs of different
          areas vary greatly making a uniform filing system
          inapplicable
       C. *desirable*, mainly because more efficient use would
          be made of filing cabinets
       D. *undesirable*, mainly because the persons using the
          files would have no discretion in organizing the
          files

22. At a social gathering, a fire officer hears a man who   22.___
describes himself as the owner of the XYZ factory state
that he *pays off* fire department inspectors who visit
his establishment. When the fire officer asks the man
whether he will repeat his statement under oath, the man
refuses with the remark, *I am not looking for trouble*.
In this situation, the fire officer should
   A. forget the incident since the factory owner isn't
      willing to give evidence
   B. investigate the background and reputation of the
      man to determine whether he really owns the factory
      and has any reason for making false statements about
      the fire department
   C. report the incident to police authorities
   D. report the incident to higher authorities in the
      fire department

23. The degree to which first-line subordinate officers will   23.___
apply the principles they learn at centralized training
sessions is PRINCIPALLY determined by the degree to which
   A. the principles are reinforced by follow-up training
      and evaluation
   B. the top echelons support these courses
   C. their immediate supervisors apply these principles
   D. the principles are useful in solving day-to-day
      problems

24. The MOST reliable of the following methods for detecting   24.___
errors in a statistical report is to
   A. compare it with reports from similar units
   B. examine it for internal inconsistency
   C. compare it with reports, from the same unit, for
      previous periods
   D. examine it for unusual or unexpected data

25. A superior officer supervising inspection duty activities   25.___
comes upon a company just as it is completing inspection
of a clothing manufacturing plant. The officer in command
reports that the company has issued minor violation orders
for five conditions which they discovered. The superior
officer considers four of the conditions cited clear violations of the Administrative Code. The fifth condition he
considers a borderline case which he, himself, would not
have handled by issuing a violation order. In this situation, the BEST of the following courses for the superior
officer to take is to
   A. direct the officer to cancel the violation order for
      the borderline situation
   B. say nothing to the officer at this time but later
      warn him against unduly strict interpretation of the
      Administrative Code
   C. accept the officer's findings without any comment at
      this time or later
   D. question the officer closely about various sections
      of the Administrative Code to determine whether he
      has a proper understanding of its requirements

KEY (CORRECT ANSWERS)

1. A		11. B
2. B		12. B
3. B		13. B
4. A		14. D
5. D		15. D
6. D		16. A
7. C		17. A
8. C		18. C
9. B		19. D
10. C		20. B

21. A
22. D
23. C
24. B
25. C

TEST 2

1. Command implies initiative and self-reliance in meeting and accepting responsibility.
   On the basis of the above statement, it follows most accurately that a fireman who attains the rank of officer is expected to
   A. recognize that self-reliance and responsibility do not extend beyond the individual
   B. assume full responsibility for the conduct of the men under his command
   C. interpret and define responsibility as identical with initiative
   D. discourage advice and suggestions concerning the performance of his duties from other members of the department
   E. extend responsibility to and promote the initiative of the men under his command

   1.___

2. The one of the following duties of a superior officer which is LEAST properly delegated to a subordinate is
   A. securing data and information for official reports
   B. preparing and completing official reports
   C. planning and organizing company operations
   D. keeping necessary and required records
   E. caring for and maintaining very expensive equipment

   2.___

3. Suppose that, as an officer, you are instructing a group of firemen on some aspect of firefighting. Of the following, the LEAST valid principle for you to observe in conducting this training is that
   A. equal emphasis should be given to every item taught
   B. practice should be realistic
   C. learning should be active rather than passive
   D. each fireman should be led to see the relationship between his own job and the jobs of other firemen
   E. practice should approach as closely as possible the real working situation

   3.___

4. Suppose that a probationary fireman assigned to your company for training is consistently below a reasonable standard of performance. Of the following, the MOST appropriate action for you to take is to
   A. advise him to apply for a transfer to another company where his work may improve
   B. determine whether the cause for his below-standard work is readily remedied

   4.___

C. assign him to an easier job which he can do more
   efficiently
D. investigate the desirability of reducing the standard
   of performance
E. ascertain precisely how far below standard his work
   falls

5. Of the following, the purpose for which you as an officer   5.___
    would LEAST frequently prefer the privacy of a personal
    conference with a fireman under your command is to
        A. discuss with him his satisfaction with his assignment
        B. determine the reasons for his frequent absences
        C. give him directions for a new assignment
        D. praise him for the excellence of his work
        E. reprimand him for an error he has made

6. Assume that you are an officer in the fire department.   6.___
    Another officer has been newly assigned to your company.
    For you to inform this newly assigned officer at an early
    opportunity of the strengths and weaknesses of the men
    placed under his command would be
        A. *desirable*; the capabilities of the firemen under the
           command of an officer may fluctuate markedly from
           day to day as a result of study and training on their
           part
        B. *undesirable*; his rapid adjustment to his new duties
           as an officer will be hindered rather than helped
        C. *desirable*; he will be able to make assignments of the
           firemen under his command to various tasks more
           intelligently
        D. *desirable*; a fireman who has made a serious error in
           the past will find it difficult to overcome his
           reputation for inefficiency
        E. *undesirable*; he can easily learn all he needs to know
           about the men under his command in a very short time

7. Of the following, the MOST valid assumption for the   7.___
    officer to make concerning the capabilities of the fire-
    men under his command is that
        A. most firemen are able to do most jobs with precisely
           the same degree of skill
        B. in general, a fireman who is not as intelligent as
           the others will be above average in mechanical
           aptitude
        C. individual differences among firemen are such that
           some men can perform certain jobs better than others
        D. the specific abilities of firemen are rarely posi-
           tively related to each other
        E. a fireman who is poor in one skill will usually show
           superior ability in other skills

8. When teaching an inexperienced fireman how to handle a   8.___
   piece of fire equipment in performing a specific operation,
   the BEST procedure for the officer to follow is to
   A. illustrate with special emphasis the wrong methods of
      performing the operation so that the fireman may avoid
      the chief pitfalls
   B. allow the fireman first to practice performing the
      operation in his own way and then gradually eliminate
      his errors
   C. explain to the fireman how to perform the operation
      and then have him repeat verbally the instructions
      until he is able to repeat them without error
   D. indicate to the fireman why the operation is impor-
      tant and then demonstrate the correct procedure
   E. describe several alternative ways of performing the
      operation and have the fireman explain why the best
      method is superior to the others

9. Upon the good judgment of the officer first at the scene   9.___
   of a fire may depend the success or failure of the depart-
   ment at that fire.
   Of the following, an action by the officer first at the
   scene of a fire which BEST illustrates the above state-
   ment is
   A. ordering an engine company to connect immediately to
      the nearest fire hydrant
   B. directing that no apparatus be parked so as to block
      the street in front of the burning building
   C. sending men in search of a fire not visible to the
      officer when the company arrives at the box from
      which the alarm was sent
   D. determining which forcible entry tools should be
      taken into the burning building
   E. determining whether more men and equipment are
      needed to fight the fire

10. The fire officer must be a leader whom his subordinates   10.___
    will follow with enthusiasm.
    The competent officer should realize that this type of
    leadership is MOST effectively based upon
    A. precisely formulated rules and regulations
    B. strong motivation on the part of the officer
    C. strict and invariable discipline
    D. respect and confidence of subordinates
    E. diligent study by both subordinates and officers

11. Of the following, the LEAST accurate statement concerning 11.___
    uniformity of action in the administration of a large
    organization is that, in general,
    A. uniformity makes for smoother and more efficient
       administration
    B. it is necessary to keep the regulations establishing
       uniformity up-to-date to meet changing conditions

C. uniformity of action assures the best possible action in every instance
D. provision should be made for exceptions to uniform action in highly unusual circumstances
E. uniformity of action is not achieved merely with the promulgation of uniform regulations

12. The most competent fireman will not necessarily make the most competent officer.
Of the following, the CHIEF implication of the above statement is that
A. an officer who does not have a good understanding of the duties of a fireman cannot command firemen effectively
B. the basic essentials of firefighting are the same for both officers and firemen
C. some traits important in an officer are not important for performing the duties of a fireman
D. if an officer is competent, it is probable that the firemen under his supervision will be competent
E. the qualities that make for a competent officer are specific and definite

12.___

13. Many officers still rely on trial and error learning.
Of the following, the CHIEF justification for trial and error learning is that it
A. saves time
B. discourages laziness
C. develops good habits of work
D. achieves the best possible method
E. gives training in problem solving

13.___

14. Suppose that, as an officer, you are instructing a group of men on a new procedure. You wish to reduce the possibility that the men will forget an important point in your lecture. Of the following, the action which is LEAST likely to help accomplish your purpose is to
A. ask at the end of the lecture whether there are any questions on any points in the lecture
B. use a demonstration to illustrate the important point
C. explain fully why this point is important to the work of the department
D. present the same point to the men in a number of different ways and from a number of different viewpoints
E. review all the important points at the end of the lecture

14.___

15. Of the following, the MOST acceptable statement dealing with the relations between officers and subordinates is that
A. if an officer is to maintain the respect of his men, he must always defend the acts of his subordinates against criticism

15.___

    B. when an order which an officer knows will make heavy
       demands on his men is to be read to them, it is a
       wise policy for him to preface the reading with some
       remarks
    C. prior approval by an officer's own superior should
       be obtained before he bestows praise on his sub-
       ordinates
    D. relationships between officers and subordinates
       should allow for no elements of personal contact
       beyond the rigid distinctions prescribed by the
       regulations
    E. disciplining subordinates in front of their fellow
       firemen is generally considered a desirable procedure

16. The variation of talents within the individual is as   16.___
    great as the variation of talents among individuals.
    Of the following, the MOST accurate statement on the
    basis of the above statement is that
    A. a person with great talent in one area will probably
       have great talent in other areas
    B. a person with little talent in one area will probably
       have little talent in other areas
    C. for any particular task, groups of individuals
       probably vary relatively little
    D. for any particular type of task, some men are
       probably much better fitted than others
    E. the ability of an individual to do a specific job
       may vary from time to time

17. Supervision is often described as a catalyst; the super-   17.___
    visor may do none of the actual work himself but effi-
    ciency is increased.
    Of the following, the BEST justification for the above
    statement is that
    A. an important phase of supervision is improvement of
       procedures
    B. good supervision requires adequate work participation
    C. a person who actively assists in a process can hardly
       be called a supervisor
    D. the quality of supervision is measured directly by
       the time required
    E. there is an optimum amount of supervision for every
       job

18. Of the following, the BEST incentive to employ in the   18.___
    supervision of a recently appointed fireman is, in
    general, to compare his present progress with
    A. the progress of the most competent fireman in the
       company
    B. the progress of the least competent fireman in the
       company
    C. the progress of the fireman of average ability in
       the company
    D. the progress of some other fireman not in the company
    E. his previous progress while in the company

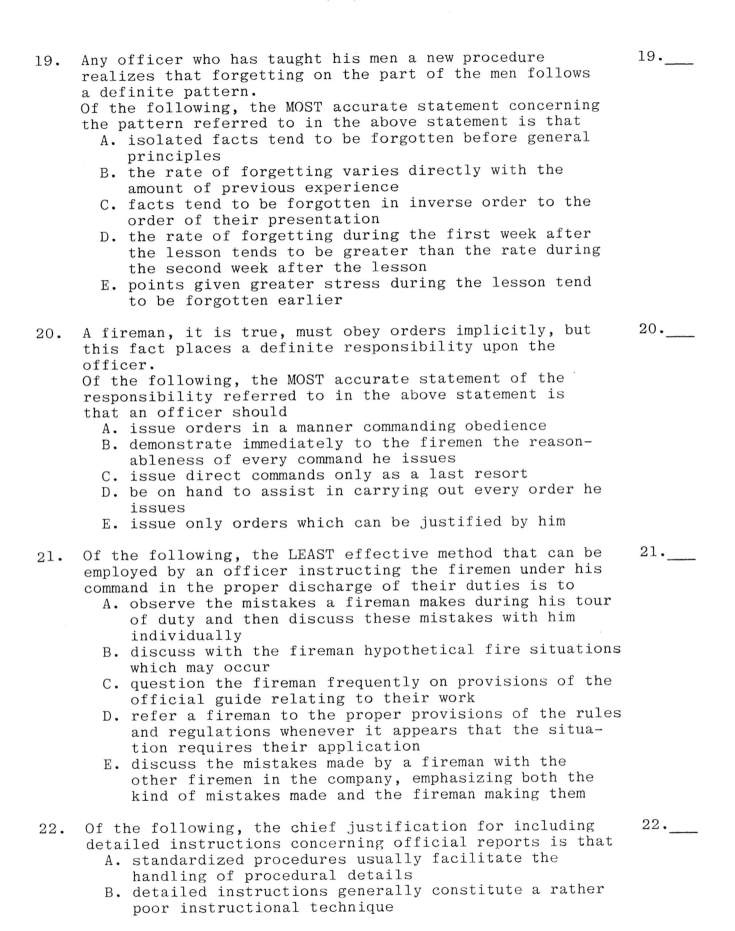

19. Any officer who has taught his men a new procedure   19.___
    realizes that forgetting on the part of the men follows
    a definite pattern.
    Of the following, the MOST accurate statement concerning
    the pattern referred to in the above statement is that
    A. isolated facts tend to be forgotten before general
       principles
    B. the rate of forgetting varies directly with the
       amount of previous experience
    C. facts tend to be forgotten in inverse order to the
       order of their presentation
    D. the rate of forgetting during the first week after
       the lesson tends to be greater than the rate during
       the second week after the lesson
    E. points given greater stress during the lesson tend
       to be forgotten earlier

20. A fireman, it is true, must obey orders implicitly, but   20.___
    this fact places a definite responsibility upon the
    officer.
    Of the following, the MOST accurate statement of the
    responsibility referred to in the above statement is
    that an officer should
    A. issue orders in a manner commanding obedience
    B. demonstrate immediately to the firemen the reason-
       ableness of every command he issues
    C. issue direct commands only as a last resort
    D. be on hand to assist in carrying out every order he
       issues
    E. issue only orders which can be justified by him

21. Of the following, the LEAST effective method that can be   21.___
    employed by an officer instructing the firemen under his
    command in the proper discharge of their duties is to
    A. observe the mistakes a fireman makes during his tour
       of duty and then discuss these mistakes with him
       individually
    B. discuss with the fireman hypothetical fire situations
       which may occur
    C. question the fireman frequently on provisions of the
       official guide relating to their work
    D. refer a fireman to the proper provisions of the rules
       and regulations whenever it appears that the situa-
       tion requires their application
    E. discuss the mistakes made by a fireman with the
       other firemen in the company, emphasizing both the
       kind of mistakes made and the fireman making them

22. Of the following, the chief justification for including   22.___
    detailed instructions concerning official reports is that
    A. standardized procedures usually facilitate the
       handling of procedural details
    B. detailed instructions generally constitute a rather
       poor instructional technique

    C. change of procedures is usually accomplished more easily when procedures are standardized

    D. every possible eventuality concerning official reports cannot be anticipated

    E. delegation of responsibility is usually facilitated if report content and procedure are clearly specified

23. Suppose that a fireman newly assigned under your command appears to lack confidence in the performance of his duties. Of the following, the BEST action for you to take is to   23.___

    A. warn him that he is being observed constantly and that the poor quality of his work is being given special consideration

    B. give him an assignment which you believe he will be able to perform well

    C. assign him to exceptionally difficult tasks which you believe will constitute a definite challenge to him

    D. have him observe the other firemen at their work for a few months until his confidence improves

    E. assign him to tasks on which he will be required to work alone

24. Accurate judgment of distances is tremendously important in firefighting.
Of the following, the BEST assumption for you to make concerning ability to judge distance is that this ability is   24.___

    A. highly variable in nature and likely to fluctuate markedly from day to day

    B. an inherited and relatively invariable trait

    C. highly correlated with intelligence

    D. highly susceptible to training

    E. likely to decline with increasing age

25. Assume that you are an officer and that a fireman with a long and excellent record in your company has recently begun to exhibit laziness and lack of interest in his work. Of the following, the BEST course of action for you as his superior officer to follow is to   25.___

    A. call the attention of the other firemen specifically to this case to demonstrate that good work requires constant, diligent application

    B. start disciplinary action immediately against this fireman as you would against any other fireman

    C. overlook the matter until the fireman again demonstrates his usual high quality of work

    D. interview the fireman and attempt to determine the reason for his unusual behavior

    E. point out to the fireman at the earliest opportunity that his excellent record is no excuse for incompetence and threaten disciplinary action unless he improves

KEY (CORRECT ANSWERS)

1. B	11. C
2. C	12. C
3. A	13. E
4. B	14. A
5. D	15. B
6. C	16. D
7. C	17. A
8. D	18. E
9. E	19. D
10. D	20. E

21. E
22. A
23. B
24. D
25. D

———

TEST 3

1. While delegation of responsibility is undesirable, delegation of authority is wise. The competent officer should realize that this statement is essentially
   A. *false*, because neither authority nor responsibility should be delegated by an officer
   B. *true*, because an officer should be responsible for his company but cannot be on hand to make all decisions
   C. *false*, because only the officer ultimately responsible for an action should be expected to make decisions
   D. *true*, because the authority of an officer is specifically set forth in the rules and regulations
   E. *true*, because each fireman is ultimately responsible for the work of his company

1.___

2. Suppose that you have assigned a task which will take several hours to a fireman under your command and have given him the appropriate instructions. About a half-hour later, you check the progress of his work and find that one specific aspect of his work is consistently incorrect. Of the following, the BEST action for you to take under these circumstances is to
   A. repeat your instructions to the fireman in full and then check the progress of his work again about a half-hour later
   B. assign that task to a fireman who you believe will perform the work more competently
   C. determine whether the fireman has correctly understood your instructions concerning the specific aspect of the work not being performed correctly
   D. observe the fireman at his work carefully for a brief period of time to determine whether you can detect the reason for his mistakes
   E. indicate to the fireman that you are dissatisfied with his work, without mentioning the nature of his errors, and wait to see whether he is sufficiently intelligent to correct his own mistakes

2.___

3. Every officer who has had occasion to teach his men how to operate a new piece of equipment has seen trial-and-error learning, in which the fireman fumbles about until he strikes upon the proper procedure by accident. Of the following, the MOST accurate statement concerning trial-and-error learning in fire training is that

3.___

    A. trial-and-error learning should be reduced by the
       officer through proper guidance
    B. the officer will find it most effective to allow
       trial-and-error learning to precede specific training
    C. trial-and-error learning is more permanent than any
       other type of learning
    D. trial-and-error learning is more efficient per unit
       time than any other type of learning
    E. interference with natural trial-and-error learning
       is likely to be wasteful and time-consuming

4. The officer is expected to train his men in all aspects of   4.___
firefighting.
Of the following, the BEST training principle for you to
follow in order to secure broad application by the firemen of the material taught to all possible types of fire
situations is that
    A. learning should be guided by the instructor
    B. insight should be developed into concepts and princi-
       ples
    C. there should be recurrent practice and review of
       learned units
    D. review should repeat original presentation in identi-
       cal form
    E. firemen should be given instruction in methods of
       teaching

5. Of the following, the CHIEF objection to allowing newly   5.___
appointed firemen under your supervision to learn correct
firefighting procedures solely on the basis of their own
experience is that a fireman
    A. rarely forgets a lesson taught by experience
    B. remembers best what he learns first
    C. learns best when he is allowed to exercise originality
    D. learns more quickly when he is guided
    E. is likely to resent an excessively domineering offi-
       cer

6. Assume that you have been appointed an officer. Of the   6.___
following, the BEST justification for learning as much
as possible about the men to be under your supervision
from the officer commanding the company to which you are
assigned is that
    A. no officer can be effective in his assignment unless
       his attitude towards the company commander is one
       of cooperation
    B. best results in handling men are usually obtained by
       treating them equally without favor
    C. some fireman often function more efficiently under
       one supervisor than under another supervisor
    D. confidence of the men in their supervisor is in-
       creased when they know he is interested in impartial
       and fair supervision
    E. effective handling of men is often based upon know-
       ledge of individual personality differences

7. Newly appointed officers will find that it is the older   7.___
   men in their companies who will be their greatest concern
   and problem.
   This statement assumes MOST directly that
       A. competence in firefighting tends to increase with
          experience
       B. strict supervision may increase the tendency on the
          part of firemen to break minor regulations
       C. the need for supervision bears little relationship
          to the amount of experience
       D. newly appointed firemen are usually less well
          acquainted with detailed regulations
       E. newly appointed firemen are so assigned that there
          are only one or two in any one company

8. In planning courses for a fireman's training program, it   8.___
   is MOST important to make the content of each lesson
   capable of being
       A. taught in one class meeting
       B. *tied* to something which the trainee already knows or
          can do
       C. spread over a number of class meetings
       D. fully learned by the trainees as something entirely
          new
       E. explained by the instructor in technical terms

9. If an officer is to be an effective leader of those under   9.___
   him, he must
       A. utilize whatever motives for work he is able to
          discern in the men working under him
       B. avoid training by direct instruction lest his men be
          deprived of initiative
       C. delegate to each man under him an equal amount of
          responsibility
       D. outline repeatedly and in great detail the work to be
          performed by each member of the group
       E. develop the assets of the men and encourage them to
          work for the good of the organization as a whole

10. When instructing firemen under his supervision, the fire   10.___
    officer should recognize the fact that
        A. learning should be uniform if instruction is the same
           for all
        B. persons differ in the amount they can learn in a
           given period of time
        C. after the age of 20 or so, a person is less capable
           of learning than before
        D. learning is seldom possible without much individual
           instruction
        E. learning should be essentially a passive procedure
           without active participation by the learner

11. Assume that you are an officer. A fireman under your   11.___
    supervision attempts to conceal the fact that he has made
    an error. You should proceed on the assumption that
    A. the evasion indicates something wrong in the funda-
       mental relationship between you and this fireman
    B. a desire for concealment indicates an antisocial
       attitude on the part of this fireman
    C. probably the fireman was merely ignorant of proper
       procedures and the entire matter is best dropped
    D. the evasion should be overlooked provided that the
       error occurred in a matter of no great importance
    E. the handling of this fireman should not be such as
       to discourage his independence of spirit

12. A good measure of the efficiency of a fire department with   12.___
    respect to fire prevention is the number of fires which
    occur per 1,000 of population.
    Of the following, the chief limitation of this suggested
    index of fire department efficiency is that
    A. the more efficient the fire department with respect
       to fire prevention the smaller the number of fires
       occurring in that area is likely to be
    B. the size of the total population in an area should
       be related to the total number of fires which occur,
       not the number which are prevented
    C. areas in which fires occur frequently may have a
       lower index of fire incidence than areas in which
       fires occur infrequently
    D. fire departments in areas which have a high rate of
       fire incidence may prevent a large number of fires
    E. the number of fires which occur varies inversely, and
       not directly, with the number of fires prevented

13. In the fire department, it is the lieutenant who is the   13.___
    key man in the enforcement of discipline.
    Of the following, the BEST justification for this state-
    ment is that
    A. the lieutenant was most recently a fireman himself,
       and so is more likely to view minor violations
       sympathetically
    B. the lieutenant, as compared with other supervisory
       officers, has a more rounded view of the operation
       of the fire department as a whole
    C. the lieutenant, as compared with other supervisory
       officers, is in closer contact with the men on the
       job
    D. if a fire department is to be well balanced, there
       should be proportionately more lieutenants than
       other supervisory officers
    E. the future chiefs and administrators in any fire
       department must necessarily be chosen from among
       the present lieutenants

14. The principle of administration that the responsibility   14.___
    of higher authority for the acts of subordinates must
    be absolute means that
      A. coordinate officers are responsible for the acts of
         each other
      B. the chief executive alone is not responsible for the
         acts of his subordinates
      C. each subordinate is held responsible for his own acts
      D. discretionary authority should not be delegated
      E. each superior officer is held responsible for all
         the acts of his subordinates

15. One of the men complains to you that you always give him   15.___
    the least desirable assignments. You should
      A. refuse to discuss the matter with him
      B. discuss the matter with him
      C. tell him that if he is dissatisfied to request a
         transfer to another company
      D. point out to him that he has not been performing his
         house duties properly
      E. bring him up on charges of insubordination

16. About a week after you have been assigned to a new   16.___
    company, you overhear two of the men making unflattering
    remarks about your ability. You should
      A. ignore the incident but review your actions of the
         past week
      B. go up to the men and discuss the matter with them in
         a friendly manner
      C. report the incident to the company commander and ask
         that either you or the men be transferred
      D. state at the next formation that you take complete
         responsibility for your acts
      E. *crack down* on these men

17. With respect to your relations with the men in the company,   17.___
    it is important for you as an officer to
      A. recognize that you have your likes and dislikes and
         to compensate for them
      B. delegate your responsibility to the men who will
         ultimately perform the work
      C. avoid having likes and dislikes
      D. restrict your relations with the men to official
         business
      E. remain as aloof as possible

18. Assume that while you are serving as an officer you   18.___
    observe a newly appointed fireman performing his house
    duties in a careless, indifferent fashion. Of the
    following actions, it is MOST desirable that you
      A. report the man to the company commander and ask him
         what to do
      B. say nothing to anyone and give the man a month or
         two to find himself

    C. show the man where his work is inadequate
    D. reprimand the man in front of the other men so that
       they can bring pressure on him
    E. ignore the matter as part of a day's work

19. As an officer, you wish to praise one of the men for
having carried out his house duties in an exemplary
manner. You should
    A. send him a letter through channels complimenting him
    B. compliment him at a formation, comparing him with
       individuals who have not been carrying their share
       of the load
    C. say nothing but give the man desirable assignments
    D. tell him what you think of his work
    E. keep this man in mind for promotion

19.___

20. You have been given the assignment to train the men of
the company in the use of a new piece of equipment. In
order to get the best results, the emphasis should be on
    A. showing them how to operate the equipment properly
       by demonstrating its operation
    B. having the men operate the equipment under your
       direct supervision
    C. teaching the complicated parts of the procedure to
       the smarter men and the simpler parts to the others
    D. having a few men learn the operation and then have
       them teach the remainder of the company
    E. the developmental lesson

20.___

21. When training a recruit, the BEST way to make him into a
capable fireman is to
    A. tell him what to do at each point so that he will
       never make a mistake
    B. encourage him to make his own decisions as far as
       his assigned duties permit
    C. refuse to answer questions to which you believe he
       should know the answers
    D. have him memorize the official guide
    E. let him strictly alone

21.___

22. A young officer can in general expect some opposition
from the older men in a company.
The one of the following in which he should be prepared
for the greatest amount of opposition is in attempting to
    A. train the men on new equipment
    B. enforce the departmental rules
    C. change the company's thinking on firefighting methods
    D. get information concerning the state of the company's
       equipment
    E. bring them together in social functions

22.___

23. As an officer, your MAJOR function is to 23.____
    A. discipline men who violate the rules and regulations of the department
    B. improve the morale of the men in the company
    C. make certain that the equipment is ready for use at all times
    D. improve the quality of the service rendered by the company
    E. improve relations with the public

24. Your company commander gives you a work assignment for 24.____
    the men which you believe to be unnecessary and which you
    know will be resented by the men. Of the following
    actions which you, as an officer, can take, it is MOST
    desirable that you
    A. make your point of view known to the company commander before carrying out his orders
    B. carry out your superior's orders without comment
    C. carry out the orders but let the men know that the orders did not originate with you
    D. change the work assignments slightly in order to make it appear more purposeful
    E. go through the motions of carrying out the assignment in order to *save face* for all concerned

25. Suppose that after you have been newly assigned to a 25.____
    company, one of the men informs you that some of the
    men are resentful of your command and plan to make things
    difficult for you. You should
    A. discuss the matter with your company commander and suggest that the clique be broken up
    B. go out of your way to be pleasant and friendly with the other men to eliminate any objections to your command
    C. thank the man and then analyze your actions and the reactions of the men in your company
    D. discuss the fancied or real grievances with other men of the company
    E. advise the man that he should not inform on others and that you can handle anyone in the company

—

KEY (CORRECT ANSWERS)

1. B	6. E	11. A	16. A	21. B
2. C	7. C	12. D	17. A	22. C
3. A	8. B	13. C	18. C	23. D
4. B	9. E	14. E	19. D	24. A
5. D	10. B	15. B	20. B	25. C

PHILOSOPHY, PRINCIPLES, PRACTICES, AND TECHNICS
OF
SUPERVISION, ADMINISTRATION, MANAGEMENT, AND ORGANIZATION

CONTENTS

CONTENTS (cont'd)

PHILOSOPHY, PRINCIPLES, PRACTICES, AND TECHNICS
OF
SUPERVISION, ADMINISTRATION, MANAGEMENT, AND ORGANIZATION

I. MEANING OF SUPERVISION

The extension of the democratic philosophy has been accompanied by an extension in the scope of supervision. Modern leaders and supervisors no longer think of supervision in the narrow sense of being confined chiefly to visiting employees, supplying materials, or rating the staff. They regard supervision as being intimately related to all the concerned agencies of society, they speak of the supervisor's function in terms of "growth", rather than the "improvement," of employees

This modern concept of supervision may be defined as follows:

Supervision is leadership and the development of leadership within groups which are cooperatively engaged in inspection, research, training, guidance and evaluation.

II. THE OLD AND THE NEW SUPERVISION

TRADITIONAL	*MODERN*
1. Inspection	1. Study and analysis
2. Focused on the employee	2. Focused on aims, materials, methods, supervisors, employees, environment
3. Visitation	3. Demonstrations, intervisitation, workshops, directed reading, bulletins, etc.
4. Random and haphazard	4. Definitely organized and planned (scientific)
5. Imposed and authoritarian	5. Cooperative and democratic
6. One person usually	6. Many persons involved (creative)

III. THE EIGHT (8) BASIC PRINCIPLES OF THE NEW SUPERVISION

1. *PRINCIPLE OF RESPONSIBILITY*

Authority to act and responsibility for acting must be joined.
   a. If you give responsibility, give authority.
   b. Define employee duties clearly.
   c. Protect employees from criticism by others.
   d. Recognize the rights as well as obligations of employees.
   e. Achieve the aims of a democratic society insofar as it is possible within the area of your work.
   f. Establish a situation favorable to training and learning.
   g. Accept ultimate responsibility for everything done in your section, unit, office, division, department.
   h. Good administration and good supervision are inseparable.

2. *PRINCIPLE OF AUTHORITY*

The success of the supervisor is measured by the extent to which the power of authority is not used.
   a. Exercise simplicity and informality in supervision.
   b. Use the simplest machinery of supervision.
   c. If it is good for the organization as a whole, it is probably justified.
   d. Seldom be arbitrary or authoritative.
   e. Do not base your work on the power of position or of personality.
   f. Permit and encourage the free expression of opinions.

3. *PRINCIPLE OF SELF-GROWTH*

The success of the supervisor is measured by the extent to which, and the speed with which, he is no longer needed.
   a. Base criticism on principles, not on specifics.
   b. Point out higher activities to employees.

c. Train for self-thinking by employees, to meet new situations.
d. Stimulate initiative, self-reliance and individual responsibility.
e. Concentrate on stimulating the growth of employees rather than on removing defects.

4. *PRINCIPLE OF INDIVIDUAL WORTH*
   Respect for the individual is a paramount consideration in supervision.
   a. Be human and sympathetic in dealing with employees.
   b. Don't nag about things to be done.
   c. Recognize the individual differences among employees and seek opportunities to permit best expression of each personality.

5. *PRINCIPLE OF CREATIVE LEADERSHIP*
   The best supervision is that which is not apparent to the employee.
   a. Stimulate, don't drive employees to creative action.
   b. Emphasize doing good things.
   c. Encourage employees to do what they do best.
   d. Do not be too greatly concerned with details of subject or method.
   e. Do not be concerned exclusively with immediate problems and activities.
   f. Reveal higher activities and make them both desired and maximally possible.
   g. Determine procedures in the light of each situation but see that these are derived from a sound basic philosophy.
   h. Aid, inspire and lead so as to liberate the creative spirit latent in all good employees.

6. *PRINCIPLE OF SUCCESS AND FAILURE*
   There are no unsuccessful employees, only unsuccessful supervisors who have failed to give proper leadership.
   a. Adapt suggestions to the capacities, attitudes, and prejudices of employees.
   b. Be gradual, be progressive, be persistent.
   c. Help the employee find the general principle; have the employee apply his own problem to the general principle.
   d. Give adequate appreciation for good work and honest effort.
   e. Anticipate employee difficulties and help to prevent them.
   f. Encourage employees to do the desirable things they will do anyway.
   g. Judge your supervision by the results it secures.

7. *PRINCIPLE OF SCIENCE*
   Successful supervision is scientific, objective, and experimental.
   It is based on facts, not on prejudices.
   a. Be cumulative in results.
   b. Never divorce your suggestions from the goals of training.
   c. Don't be impatient of results.
   d. Keep all matters on a professional, not a personal level.
   e. Do not be concerned exclusively with immediate problems and activities.
   f. Use objective means of determining achievement and rating where possible.

8. *PRINCIPLE OF COOPERATION*
   Supervision is a cooperative enterprise between supervisor and employee.
   a. Begin with conditions as they are.
   b. Ask opinions of all involved when formulating policies.

c. Organization is as good as its weakest link.
d. Let employees help to determine policies and department programs.
e. Be approachable and accessible - physically and mentally.
f. Develop pleasant social relationships.

IV. WHAT IS ADMINISTRATION?

Administration is concerned with providing the environment, the material facilities, and the operational procedures that will promote the maximum growth and development of supervisors and employees. (Organization is an aspect, and a concomitant, of administration.)

There is no sharp line of demarcation between supervision and administration; these functions are intimately interrelated and, often, overlapping. They are complementary activities.

1. *PRACTICES COMMONLY CLASSED AS "SUPERVISORY"*
   a. Conducting employees conferences
   b. Visiting sections, units, offices, divisions, departments
   c. Arranging for demonstrations
   d. Examining plans
   e. Suggesting professional reading
   f. Interpreting bulletins
   g. Recommending in-service training courses
   h. Encouraging experimentation
   i. Appraising employee morale
   j. Providing for intervisitation
2. *PRACTICES COMMONLY CLASSIFIED AS "ADMINISTRATIVE"*
   a. Management of the office
   b. Arrangement of schedules for extra duties
   c. Assignment of rooms or areas
   d. Distribution of supplies
   e. Keeping records and reports
   f. Care of audio-visual materials
   g. Keeping inventory records
   h. Checking record cards and books
   i. Programming special activities
   j. Checking on the attendance and punctuality of employees
3. *PRACTICES COMMONLY CLASSIFIED AS BOTH "SUPERVISORY" AND "ADMINISTRATIVE"*
   a. Program construction
   b. Testing or evaluating outcomes
   c. Personnel accounting
   d. Ordering instructional materials

V. RESPONSIBILITIES OF THE SUPERVISOR

A person employed in a supervisory capacity must constantly be able to improve his own efficiency and ability. He represents the employer to the employees and only continuous self-examination can make him a capable supervisor.

Leadership and training are the supervisor's responsibility. An efficient working unit is one in which the employees work with the supervisor. It is his job to bring out the best in his employees. He must always be relaxed, courteous and calm in his association with his employees. Their feelings are important, and a harsh attitude does not develop the most efficient employees.

VI. COMPETENCIES OF THE SUPERVISOR

1. Complete knowledge of the duties and responsibilities of his position.
2. To be able to organize a job, plan ahead and carry through.
3. To have self-confidence and initiative.
4. To be able to handle the unexpected situation and make quick decisions.
5. To be able to properly train subordinates in the positions they are best suited for.
6. To be able to keep good human relations among his subordinates.
7. To be able to keep good human relations between his subordinates and himself and to earn their respect and trust.

VII. THE PROFESSIONAL SUPERVISOR-EMPLOYEE RELATIONSHIP

There are two kinds of efficiency: one kind is only apparent and is produced in organizations through the exercise of mere discipline; this is but a simulation of the second, or true, efficiency which springs from spontaneous cooperation. If you are a manager, no matter how great or small your responsibility, it is your job, in the final analysis, to create and develop this involuntary cooperation among the people whom you supervise. For, no matter how powerful a combination of money, machines, and materials a company may have, this is a dead and sterile thing without a team of willing, thinking and articulate people to guide it.

The following 21 points are presented as indicative of the exemplary basic relationship that should exist between supervisor and employee:

1. Each person wants to be liked and respected by his fellow employee and wants to be treated with consideration and respect by his superior.
2. The most competent employee will make an error. However, in a unit where good relations exist between the supervisor and his employees, tenseness and fear do not exist. Thus, errors are not hidden or covered up and the efficiency of a unit is not impaired.
3. Subordinates resent rules, regulations, or orders that are unreasonable or unexplained.
4. Subordinates are quick to resent unfairness, harshness, injustices and favoritism.
5. An employee will accept responsibility if he knows that he will be complimented for a job well done, and not too harshly chastized for failure; that his supervisor will check the cause of the failure, and, if it was the supervisor's fault, he will assume the blame therefor. If it was the employee's fault, his supervisor will explain the correct method or means of handling the responsibility.
6. An employee wants to receive credit for a suggestion he has made, that is used. If a suggestion cannot be used, the employee is entitled to an explanation. The supervisor should not say "no" and close the subject.
7. Fear and worry slow up a worker's ability. Poor working environment can impair his physical and mental health. A good supervisor avoids forceful methods, threats and arguments to get a job done.
8. A forceful supervisor is able to train his employees individually and as a team, and is able to motivate them in the proper channels.

9. A mature supervisor is able to properly evaluate his subordinates and to keep them happy and satisfied.
10. A sensitive supervisor will never patronize his subordinates.
11. A worthy supervisor will respect his employees' confidences.
12. Definite and clear-cut responsibilities should be assigned to each executive.
13. Responsibility should always be coupled with corresponding authority.
14. No change should be made in the scope or responsibilities of a position without a definite understanding to that effect on the part of all persons concerned.
15. No executive or employee, occupying a single position in the organization, should be subject to definite orders from more than one source.
16. Orders should never be given to subordinates over the head of a responsible executive. Rather than do this, the officer in question should be supplanted.
17. Criticisms of subordinates should, whever possible, be made privately, and in no case should a subordinate be criticized in the presence of executives or employees of equal or lower rank.
18. No dispute or difference between executives or employees as to authority or responsibilities should be considered too trivial for prompt and careful adjudication.
19. Promotions, wage changes, and disciplinary action should always be approved by the executive immediately superior to the one directly responsible.
20. No executive or employee should ever be required, or expected, to be at the same time an assistant to, and critic of, another.
21. Any executive whose work is subject to regular inspection should, whever practicable, be given the assistance and facilities necessary to enable him to maintain an independent check of the quality of his work.

VIII. MINI-TEXT IN SUPERVISION, ADMINISTRATION, MANAGEMENT, AND ORGANIZATION

A. BRIEF HIGHLIGHTS

Listed concisely and sequentially are major headings and important data in the field for quick recall and review.

1. *LEVELS OF MANAGEMENT*

Any organization of some size has several levels of management. In terms of a ladder the levels are:

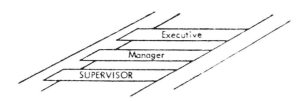

The first level is very important because it is the beginning point of management leadership.

2. *WHAT THE SUPERVISOR MUST LEARN*

A supervisor must learn to:
   (1) Deal with people and their differences
   (2) Get the job done through people
   (3) Recognize the problems when they exist
   (4) Overcome obstacles to good performance
   (5) Evaluate the performance of people
   (6) Check his own performance in terms of accomplishment

3. *A DEFINITION OF SUPERVISOR*
      The term supervisor means any individual having authority, in the interests of the employer, to hire,transfer,suspend,lay-off,recall, promote,discharge,assign,reward,or discipline other employees... or responsibility to direct them,or to adjust their grievances,or effectively to recommend such action,if, in connection with the foregoing, exercise of such authority is not of a merely routine or clerical nature but requires the use of independent judgment.
4. *ELEMENTS OF THE TEAM CONCEPT*
      What is involved in teamwork? The component parts are:
      (1) Members   (3) Goals   (5) Cooperation
      (2) A leader   (4) Plans   (6) Spirit
5. *PRINCIPLES OF ORGANIZATION*
      (1) A team member must know what his job is
      (2) Be sure that the nature and scope of a job are understood
      (3) Authority and responsibility should be carefully spelled out
      (4) A supervisor should be permitted to make the maximum number of decisions affecting his employees
      (5) Employees should report to only one supervisor
      (6) A supervisor should direct only as many employees as he can handle effectively
      (7) An organization plan should be flexible
      (8) Inspection and performance of work should be separate
      (9) Organizational problems should receive immediate attention
      (10) Assign work in line with ability and experience
6. *THE FOUR IMPORTANT PARTS OF EVERY JOB*
      (1) Inherent in every job is the *accountability* for results
      (2) A second set of factors in every job are *responsibilities*
      (3) Along with duties and responsibilities one must have the *authority* to act within certain limits without obtaining permission to proceed
      (4) No job exists in a vacuum. The supervisor is surrounded by key *relationships*
7. *PRINCIPLES OF DELEGATION*
      Where work is delegated for the first time,the supervisor should think in terms of these questions:
      (1) Who is best qualified to do this?
      (2) Can an employee improve his abilities by doing this?
      (3) How long should an employee spend on this?
      (4) Are there any special problems for which he will need guidance?
      (5) How broad a delegation can I make?
8. *PRINCIPLES OF EFFECTIVE COMMUNICATIONS*
      (1) Determine the media
      (2) To whom directed?
      (3) Identification and source authority
      (4) Is communication understood?
9. *PRINCIPLES OF WORK IMPROVEMENT*
      (1) Most people usually do only the work which is assigned to them
      (2) Workers are likely to fit assigned work into the time available to perform it
      (3) A good workload usually stimulates output
      (4) People usually do their best work when they know that results will be reviewed or inspected

    (5) Employees usually feel that someone else is responsible for conditions of work, workplace layout, job methods, type of tools and equipment, and other such factors

    (6) Employees are usually defensive about their job security

    (7) Employees have natural resistance to change

    (8) Employees can support or destroy a supervisor

    (9) A supervisor usually earns the respect of his people through his personal example of diligence and efficiency

10. *AREAS OF JOB IMPROVEMENT*

  The *areas* of job improvement are quite numerous, but the most common ones which a supervisor can identify and utilize are:

    (1) Departmental layout   (5) Work methods
    (2) Flow of work   (6) Materials handling
    (3) Workplace layout   (7) Utilization
    (4) Utilization of manpower (8) Motion economy

11. *SEVEN KEY POINTS IN MAKING IMPROVEMENTS*

    (1) Select the job to be improved
    (2) Study how it is being done now
    (3) Question the present method
    (4) Determine actions to be taken
    (5) Chart proposed method
    (6) Get approval and apply
    (7) Solicit worker participation

12. *CORRECTIVE TECHNIQUES OF JOB IMPROVEMENT*

Specific Problems	*General Problems*	*Corrective Technique*
(1) Size of workload	(1) Departmental layout	(1) Study with scale model
(2) Inability to meet schedules	(2) Flow of work	(2) Flow chart study
(3) Strain and fatigue	(3) Workplan layout	(3) Motion analysis
(4) Improper use of men and skills	(4) Utilization of manpower	(4) Comparison of units produced to standard allowances
(5) Waste, poor quality, unsafe conditions	(5) Work methods	(5) Methods analysis
(6) Bottleneck conditions that hinder output	(6) Materials handling	(6) Flow chart and equipment study
(7) Poor utilization of equipment and machines	(7) Utilization of equipment	(7) Down time vs. running time
(8) Efficiency and productivity of labor	(8) Motion economy	(8) Motion analysis

13. *A PLANNING CHECKLIST*

    (1) Objectives   (8) Equipment
    (2) Controls   (9) Supplies and materials
    (3) Delegations   (10) Utilization of time
    (4) Communications (11) Safety
    (5) Resources   (12) Money
    (6) Methods and procedures (13) Work
    (7) Manpower   (14) Timing of improvements

14. *FIVE CHARACTERISTICS OF GOOD DIRECTIONS*

  In order to get results, directions must be:

    (1) Possible of accomplishment (4) Planned and complete
    (2) Agreeable with worker interests (5) Unmistakably clear
    (3) Related to mission

15. *TYPES OF DIRECTIONS*
      (1) Demands or direct orders   (3) Suggestion or implication
      (2) Requests   (4) Volunteering

16. *CONTROLS*
   A typical listing of the overall areas in which the supervisor should establish controls might be:
      (1) Manpower   (4) Quantity of work (7) Money
      (2) Materials   (5) Time   (8) Methods
      (3) Quality of work (6) Space

17. *ORIENTING THE NEW EMPLOYEE*
      (1) Prepare for him   (3) Orientation for the job
      (2) Welcome the new employee (4) Follow-up

18. *CHECKLIST FOR ORIENTING NEW EMPLOYEES*

Yes No

      (1) Do your appreciate the feelings of new employees when they first report for work? ... ...
      (2) Are you aware of the fact that the new employee must make a big adjustment to his job? ... ...
      (3) Have you given him good reasons for liking the job and the organization? ... ...
      (4) Have you prepared for his first day on the job? ... ...
      (5) Did you welcome him cordially and make him feel needed? ... ...
      (6) Did you establish rapport with him so that he feels free to talk and discuss matters with you?... ...
      (7) Did you explain his job to him and his relationship to you? ... ...
      (8) Does he know that his work will be evaluated periodically on a basis that is fair and objective?.. ...
      (9) Did you introduce him to his fellow workers in such a way that they are likely to accept him? ... ...
   (10) Does he know what employee benefits he will receive? ... ...
   (11) Does he understand the importance of being on the job and what to do if he must leave his duty station? ... ...
   (12) Has he been impressed with the importance of accident prevention and safe practice? ... ...
   (13) Does he generally know his way around the department? ... ...
   (14) Is he under the guidance of a sponsor who will teach the right ways of doing things? ... ...
   (15) Do you plan to follow-up so that he will continue to adjust successfully to his job? ... ...

19. *PRINCIPLES OF LEARNING*
      (1) Motivation (2) Demonstration or explanation
      (3) Practice

20. *CAUSES OF POOR PERFORMANCE*
      (1) Improper training for job (6) Lack of standards of
      (2) Wrong tools   performance
      (3) Inadequate directions   (7) Wrong work habits
      (4) Lack of supervisory follow-up(8) Low morale
      (5) Poor communications   (9) Other

21. *FOUR MAJOR STEPS IN ON-THE-JOB INSTRUCTION*
      (1) Prepare the worker   (3) Tryout performance
      (2) Present the operation   (4) Follow-up

22. *EMPLOYEES WANT FIVE THINGS*
    (1) Security   (2) Opportunity   (3) Recognition
    (4) Inclusion   (5) Expression
23. *SOME DON'TS IN REGARD TO PRAISE*
    (1) Don't praise a person for something he hasn't done
    (2) Don't praise a person unless you can be sincere
    (3) Don't be sparing in praise just because your superior withholds it from you
    (4) Don't let too much time elapse between good performance and recognition of it
24. *HOW TO GAIN YOUR WORKERS' CONFIDENCE*
    Methods of developing confidence include such things as:
    (1) Knowing the interests, habits, hobbies of employees
    (2) Admitting your own inadequacies
    (3) Sharing and telling of confidence in others
    (4) Supporting people when they are in trouble
    (5) Delegating matters that can be well handled
    (6) Being frank and straightforward about problems and working conditions
    (7) Encouraging others to bring their problems to you
    (8) Taking action on problems which impede worker progress
25. *SOURCES OF EMPLOYEE PROBLEMS*
    On-the-job causes might be such things as:
    (1) A feeling that favoritism is exercised in assignments
    (2) Assignment of overtime
    (3) An undue amount of supervision
    (4) Changing methods or systems
    (5) Stealing of ideas or trade secrets
    (6) Lack of interest in job
    (7) Threat of reduction in force
    (8) Ignorance or lack of communications
    (9) Poor equipment
    (10) Lack of knowing how supervisor feels toward employee
    (11) Shift assignments
    Off-the-job problems might have to do with:
    (1) Health (2) Finances (3) Housing (4) Family
26. *THE SUPERVISOR'S KEY TO DISCIPLINE*
    There are several key points about discipline which the supervisor should keep in mind:
    (1) Job discipline is one of the disciplines of life and is directed by the supervisor.
    (2) It is more important to correct an employee fault than to fix blame for it.
    (3) Employee performance is affected by problems both on the job and off.
    (4) Sudden or abrupt changes in behavior can be indications of important employee problems.
    (5) Problems should be dealt with as soon as possible after they are identified.
    (6) The attitude of the supervisor may have more to do with solving problems than the techniques of problem solving.
    (7) Correction of employee behavior should be resorted to only after the supervisor is sure that training or counseling will not be helpful
    (8) Be sure to document your disciplinary actions.

   (9) Make sure that you are disciplining on the basis of facts rather than personal feelings.

   (10) Take each disciplinary step in order, being careful not to make snap judgments, or decisions based on impatience.

27. *FIVE IMPORTANT PROCESSES OF MANAGEMENT*

   (1) Planning   (2) Organizing   (3) Scheduling

   (4) Controlling   (5) Motivating

28. *WHEN THE SUPERVISOR FAILS TO PLAN*

   (1) Supervisor creates impression of not knowing his job

   (2) May lead to excessive overtime

   (3) Job runs itself-- supervisor lacks control

   (4) Deadlines and appointments missed

   (5) Parts of the work go undone

   (6) Work interrupted by emergencies

   (7) Sets a bad example

   (8) Uneven workload creates peaks and valleys

   (9) Too much time on minor details at expense of more important tasks

29. *FOURTEEN GENERAL PRINCIPLES OF MANAGEMENT*

   (1) Division of work   (8) Centralization

   (2) Authority and responsibility (9) Scalar chain

   (3) Discipline   (10) Order

   (4) Unity of command   (11) Equity

   (5) Unity of direction   (12) Stability of tenure of

   (6) Subordination of individual   personnel

    interest to general interest(13) Initiative

   (7) Remuneration of personnel (14) Esprit de corps

30. *CHANGE*

 Bringing about change is perhaps attempted more often, and yet less well understood, than anything else the supervisor does. How do people generally react to change? (People tend to resist change that is imposed upon them by other individuals or circumstances.)

 Change is characteristic of every situation. It is a part of every real endeavor where the efforts of people are concerned.

  A. Why do people resist change?

   People may resist change because of:

    (1) Fear of the unknown

    (2) Implied criticism

    (3) Unpleasant experiences in the past

    (4) Fear of loss of status

    (5) Threat to the ego

    (6) Fear of loss of economic stability

  B. How can we best overcome the resistance to change?

   In initiating change, take these steps:

    (1) Get ready to sell

    (2) identify sources of help

    (3) Anticipate objections

    (4) Sell benefits

    (5) Listen in depth

    (6) Follow up

B. BRIEF TOPICAL SUMMARIES

I. WHO/WHAT IS THE SUPERVISOR?
  1. The supervisor is often called the "highest level employee and the lowest level manager."
  2. A supervisor is a member of both management and the work group. He acts as a bridge between the two.
  3. Most problems in supervision are in the area of human relations, or people problems.
  4. Employees expect: Respect, opportunity to learn and to advance, and a sense of belonging, and so forth.
  5. Supervisors are responsible for directing people and organizing work. Planning is of paramount importance.
  6. A position description is a set of duties and responsibilities inherent to a given position.
  7. It is important to keep the position description up-to-date and to provide each employee with his own copy.

II. THE SOCIOLOGY OF WORK
  1. People are alike in many ways; however each individual is unique.
  2. The supervisor is challenged in getting to know employee differences. Acquiring skills in evaluating individuals is an asset.
  3. Maintaining meaningful working relationships in the organization is of great importance.
  4. The supervisor has an obligation to help individuals to develop to their fullest potential.
  5. Job rotation on a planned basis helps to build versatility and to maintain interest and enthusiasm in work groups.
  6. Cross training (job rotation) provides backup skills.
  7. The supervisor can help reduce tension by maintaining a sense of humor, providing guidance to employees, and by making reasonable and timely decisions. Employees respond favorably to working under reasonably predictable circumstances.
  8. Change is characteristic of all managerial behavior. The supervisor must adjust to changes in procedures, new methods, technological changes, and to a number of new and sometimes challenging situations.
  9. To overcome the natural tendency for people to resist change, the supervisor should become more skillful in initiating change.

II. PRINCIPLES AND PRACTICES OF SUPERVISION
  1. Employees should be required to answer to only one superior.
  2. A supervisor can effectively direct only a limited number of employees, depending upon the complexity, variety, and proximity of the jobs involved.
  3. The organizational chart presents the organization in graphic form. It reflects lines of authority and responsibility as well as interrelationships of units within the organization.
  4. Distribution of work can be improved through an analysis using the "Work Distribution Chart."
  5. The "Work Distribution Chart" reflects the division of work within a unit in understandable form.
  6. When related tasks are given to an employee, he has a better chance of increasing his skills through training.
  7. The individual who is given the responsibility for tasks must also be given the appropriate authority to insure adequate results.
  8. The supervisor should delegate repetitive, routine work. Preparation of recurring reports, maintaining leave and attendance records are some examples.

9. Good discipline is essential to good task performance. Discipline is reflected in the actions of employees on the job in the absence of supervision.

10. Disciplinary action may have to be taken when the positive aspects of discipline have failed. Reprimand, warning, and suspension are examples of disciplinary action.

11. If a situation calls for a reprimand, be sure it is deserved and remember it is to be done in private.

IV. DYNAMIC LEADERSHIP

1. A style is a personal method or manner of exerting influence.

2. Authoritarian leaders often see themselves as the source of power and authority.

3. The democratic leader often perceives the group as the source of authority and power.

4. Supervisors tend to do better when using the pattern of leadership that is most natural for them.

5. Social scientists suggest that the effective supervisor use the leadership style that best fits the problem or circumstances involved.

6. All four styles -- telling, selling, consulting, joining -- have their place. Using one does not preclude using the other at another time.

7. The theory X point of view assumes that the average person dislikes work, will avoid it whenever possible, and must be coerced to achieve organizational objectives.

8. The theory Y point of view assumes that the average person considers work to be as natural as play, and, when the individual is committed, he requires little supervision or direction to accomplish desired objectives.

9. The leader's basic assumptions concerning human behavior and human nature affect his actions, decisions, and other managerial practices.

10. Dissatisfaction among employees is often present, but difficult to isolate. The supervisor should seek to weaken dissatisfaction by keeping promises, being sincere and considerate, keeping employees informed, and so forth.

11. Constructive suggestions should be encouraged during the natural progress of the work.

V. PROCESSES FOR SOLVING PROBLEMS

1. People find their daily tasks more meaningful and satisfying when they can improve them.

2. The causes of problems, or the key factors, are often hidden in the background. Ability to solve problems often involves the ability to isolate them from their backgrounds. There is some substance to the cliché that some persons "can't see the forest for the trees."

3. New procedures are often developed from old ones. Problems should be broken down into manageable parts. New ideas can be adapted from old ones.

4. People think differently in problem-solving situations. Using a logical, patterned approach is often useful. One approach found to be useful includes these steps:
   (a) Define the problem   (d) Weigh and decide
   (b) Establish objectives   (e) Take action
   (c) Get the facts   (f) Evaluate action

VI. TRAINING FOR RESULTS

1. Participants respond best when they feel training is important to them.
2. The supervisor has responsibility for the training and development of those who report to him.
3. When training is delegated to others, great care must be exercised to insure the trainer has knowledge, aptitude, and interest for his work as a trainer.
4. Training (learning) of some type goes on continually. The most successful supervisor makes certain the learning contributes in a productive manner to operational goals.
5. New employees are particularly susceptible to training. Older employees facing new job situations require specific training, as well as having need for development and growth opportunities.
6. Training needs require continuous monitoring.
7. The training officer of an agency is a professional with a responsibility to assist supervisors in solving training problems.
8. Many of the self-development steps important to the supervisor's own growth are equally important to the development of peers and subordinates. Knowledge of these is important when the supervisor consults with others on development and growth opportunities.

VII. HEALTH, SAFETY, AND ACCIDENT PREVENTION

1. Management-minded supervisors take appropriate measures to assist employees in maintaining health and in assuring safe practices in the work environment.
2. Effective safety training and practices help to avoid injury and accidents.
3. Safety should be a management goal. All infractions of safety which are observed should be corrected without exception.
4. Employees' safety attitude, training and instruction, provision of safe tools and equipment, supervision, and leadership are considered highly important factors which contribute to safety and which can be influenced directly by supervisors.
5. When accidents do occur they should be investigated promptly for very important reasons, including the fact that information which is gained can be used to prevent accidents in the future.

III. EQUAL EMPLOYMENT OPPORTUNITY

1. The supervisor should endeavor to treat all employees fairly, without regard to religion, race, sex, or national origin.
2. Groups tend to reflect the attitude of the leader. Prejudice can be detected even in very subtle form. Supervisors must strive to create a feeling of mutual respect and confidence in every employee.
3. Complete utilization of all human resources is a national goal. Equitable consideration should be accorded women in the work force, minority-group members, the physically and mentally handicapped, and the older employee. The important question is: "Who can do the job?"
4. Training opportunities, recognition for performance, overtime assignments, promotional opportunities, and all other personnel actions are to be handled on an equitable basis.

IX. IMPROVING COMMUNICATIONS

1. Communications is achieving understanding between the sender and the receiver of a message. It also means sharing information -- the creation of understanding.
2. Communication is basic to all human activity. Words are means of conveying meanings; however, real meanings are in people.
3. There are very practical differences in the effectiveness of one-way, impersonal, and two-way communications. Words spoken face-to-face are better understood. Telephone conversations are effective, but lack the rapport of person-to-person exchanges. The whole person communicates.
4. Cooperation and communication in an organization go hand-in-hand. When there is a mutual respect between people, spelling out rules and procedures for communicating is unnecessary.
5. There are several barriers to effective communications. These include failure to listen with respect and understanding, lack of skill in feedback, and misinterpreting the meanings of words used by the speaker. It is also common practice to listen to what we want to hear, and tune out things we do not want to hear.
6. Communication is management's chief problem. The supervisor should accept the challenge to communicate more effectively and to improve interagency and intra-agency communications.
7. The supervisor may often plan for and conduct meetings. The planning phase is critical and may determine the success or the failure of a meeting.
8. Speaking before groups usually requires extra effort. Stage fright may never disappear completely, but it can be controlled.

X. SELF-DEVELOPMENT

1. Every employee is responsible for his own self-development.
2. Toastmaster and toastmistress clubs offer opportunities to improve skills in oral communications.
3. Planning for one's own self-development is of vital importance. Supervisors know their own strengths and limitations better than anyone else.
4. Many opportunities are open to aid the supervisor in his developmental efforts, including job assignments; training opportunities, both governmental and non-governmental -- to include universities and professional conferences and seminars.
5. Programmed instruction offers a means of studying at one's own rate.
6. Where difficulties may arise from a supervisor's being away from his work for training, he may participate in televised home study or correspondence courses to meet his self-development needs.

XI. TEACHING AND TRAINING

A. The Teaching Process

Teaching is encouraging and guiding the learning activities of students toward established goals. In most cases this process consists in five steps: preparation, presentation, summarization, evaluation, and application.

1. Preparation

   Preparation is twofold in nature; that of the supervisor and the employee.

   Preparation by the supervisor is absolutely essential to success. He must know what, when, where, how, and whom he will teach. Some of the factors that should be considered are:

   (1) The objectives   (5) Employee interest
   (2) The materials needed   (6) Training aids
   (3) The methods to be used   (7) Evaluation
   (4) Employee participation   (8) Summarization

   Employee preparation consists in preparing the employee to receive the material. Probably the most important single factor in the preparation of the employee is arousing and maintaining his interest. He must know the objectives of the training, why he is there, how the material can be used, and its importance to him.

2. Presentation

   In presentation, have a carefully designed plan and follow it. The plan should be accurate and complete, yet flexible enough to meet situations as they arise. The method of presentation will be determined by the particular situation and objectives.

3. Summary

   A summary should be made at the end of every training unit and program. In addition, there may be internal summaries depending on the nature of the material being taught. The important thing is that the trainee must always be able to understand how each part of the new material relates to the whole.

4. Application

   The supervisor must arrange work so the employee will be given a chance to apply new knowledge or skills while the material is still clear in his mind and interest is high. The trainee does not really know whether he has learned the material until he has been given a chance to apply it. If the material is not applied, it loses most of its value.

5. Evaluation

   The purpose of all training is to promote learning. To determine whether the training has been a success or failure, the supervisor must evaluate this learning.

   In the broadest sense evaluation includes all the devices, methods, skills, and techniques used by the supervisor to keep himself and the employees informed as to their progress toward the objectives they are pursuing. The extent to which the employee has mastered the knowledge, skills, and abilities, or changed his attitudes, as determined by the program objectives, is the extent to which instruction has succeeded or failed.

   Evaluation should not be confined to the end of the lesson, day, or program but should be used continuously. We shall note later the way this relates to the rest of the teaching process.

B. Teaching Methods

   A teaching method is a pattern of identifiable student and instructor activity used in presenting training material.

   All supervisors are faced with the problem of deciding which method should be used at a given time.

1. Lecture
   The lecture is direct oral presentation of material by the supervisor. The present trend is to place less emphasis on the trainer's activity and more on that of the trainee.
2. Discussion
   Teaching by discussion or conference involves using questions and other techniques to arouse interest and focus attention upon certain areas, and by doing so creating a learning situation. This can be one of the most valuable methods because it gives the employees an opportunity to express their ideas and pool their knowledge.
3. Demonstration
   The demonstration is used to teach how something works or how to do something. It can be used to show a principle or what the results of a series of actions will be. A well-staged demonstration is particularly effective because it shows proper methods of performance in a realistic manner.
4. Performance
   Performance is one of the most fundamental of all learning techniques or teaching methods. The trainee may be able to tell how a specific operation should be performed but he cannot be sure he knows how to perform the operation until he has done so.

As with all methods, there are certain advantages and disadvantages to each method.

5. Which Method to Use
   Moreover, there are other methods and techniques of teaching. It is difficult to use any method without other methods entering into it. In any learning situation a combination of methods is usually more effective than any one method alone.

Finally, evaluation must be integrated into the other aspects of the teaching-learning process.

It must be used in the motivation of the trainees; it must be used to assist in developing understanding during the training; and it must be related to employee application of the results of training.

This is distinctly the role of the supervisor.

———

ANSWER SHEET

TEST NO. _____ PART _____ TITLE OF POSITION _____

(AS GIVEN IN EXAMINATION ANNOUNCEMENT - INCLUDE OPTION, IF ANY)

PLACE OF EXAMINATION _____ DATE _____

(CITY OR TOWN)   (STATE)

RATING

USE THE SPECIAL PENCIL. MAKE GLOSSY BLACK MARKS.

	A	B	C	D	E			A	B	C	D	E			A	B	C	D	E			A	B	C	D	E			A	B	C	D	E
1							26							51							76							101					
2							27							52							77							102					
3							28							53							78							103					
4							29							54							79							104					
5							30							55							80							105					
6							31							56							81							106					
7							32							57							82							107					
8							33							58							83							108					
9							34							59							84							109					
10							35							60							85							110					

Make only ONE mark for each answer.   Additional and stray marks may be counted as mistakes.   In making corrections, erase errors COMPLETELY.

	A	B	C	D	E			A	B	C	D	E			A	B	C	D	E			A	B	C	D	E			A	B	C	D	E
11							36							61							86							111					
12							37							62							87							112					
13							38							63							88							113					
14							39							64							89							114					
15							40							65							90							115					
16							41							66							91							116					
17							42							67							92							117					
18							43							68							93							118					
19							44							69							94							119					
20							45							70							95							120					
21							46							71							96							121					
22							47							72							97							122					
23							48							73							98							123					
24							49							74							99							124					
25							50							75							100							125					

ANSWER SHEET

TEST NO. _____ PART _____ TITLE OF POSITION _____
(AS GIVEN IN EXAMINATION ANNOUNCEMENT - INCLUDE OPTION, IF ANY)

PLACE OF EXAMINATION _____ DATE_____
(CITY OR TOWN)   (STATE)

RATING

USE THE SPECIAL PENCIL. MAKE GLOSSY BLACK MARKS.

	A B C D E		A B C D E		A B C D E		A B C D E		A B C D E
1	┊ ┊ ┊ ┊ ┊	26	┊ ┊ ┊ ┊ ┊	51	┊ ┊ ┊ ┊ ┊	76	┊ ┊ ┊ ┊ ┊	101	┊ ┊ ┊ ┊ ┊
2	┊ ┊ ┊ ┊ ┊	27	┊ ┊ ┊ ┊ ┊	52	┊ ┊ ┊ ┊ ┊	77	┊ ┊ ┊ ┊ ┊	102	┊ ┊ ┊ ┊ ┊
3	┊ ┊ ┊ ┊ ┊	28	┊ ┊ ┊ ┊ ┊	53	┊ ┊ ┊ ┊ ┊	78	┊ ┊ ┊ ┊ ┊	103	┊ ┊ ┊ ┊ ┊
4	┊ ┊ ┊ ┊ ┊	29	┊ ┊ ┊ ┊ ┊	54	┊ ┊ ┊ ┊ ┊	79	┊ ┊ ┊ ┊ ┊	104	┊ ┊ ┊ ┊ ┊
5	┊ ┊ ┊ ┊ ┊	30	┊ ┊ ┊ ┊ ┊	55	┊ ┊ ┊ ┊ ┊	80	┊ ┊ ┊ ┊ ┊	105	┊ ┊ ┊ ┊ ┊
6	┊ ┊ ┊ ┊ ┊	31	┊ ┊ ┊ ┊ ┊	56	┊ ┊ ┊ ┊ ┊	81	┊ ┊ ┊ ┊ ┊	106	┊ ┊ ┊ ┊ ┊
7	┊ ┊ ┊ ┊ ┊	32	┊ ┊ ┊ ┊ ┊	57	┊ ┊ ┊ ┊ ┊	82	┊ ┊ ┊ ┊ ┊	107	┊ ┊ ┊ ┊ ┊
8	┊ ┊ ┊ ┊ ┊	33	┊ ┊ ┊ ┊ ┊	58	┊ ┊ ┊ ┊ ┊	83	┊ ┊ ┊ ┊ ┊	108	┊ ┊ ┊ ┊ ┊
9	┊ ┊ ┊ ┊ ┊	34	┊ ┊ ┊ ┊ ┊	59	┊ ┊ ┊ ┊ ┊	84	┊ ┊ ┊ ┊ ┊	109	┊ ┊ ┊ ┊ ┊
10	┊ ┊ ┊ ┊ ┊	35	┊ ┊ ┊ ┊ ┊	60	┊ ┊ ┊ ┊ ┊	85	┊ ┊ ┊ ┊ ┊	110	┊ ┊ ┊ ┊ ┊

Make only ONE mark for each answer. Additional and stray marks may be
counted as mistakes. In making corrections, erase errors COMPLETELY.

	A B C D E		A B C D E		A B C D E		A B C D E		A B C D E
11	┊ ┊ ┊ ┊ ┊	36	┊ ┊ ┊ ┊ ┊	61	┊ ┊ ┊ ┊ ┊	86	┊ ┊ ┊ ┊ ┊	111	┊ ┊ ┊ ┊ ┊
12	┊ ┊ ┊ ┊ ┊	37	┊ ┊ ┊ ┊ ┊	62	┊ ┊ ┊ ┊ ┊	87	┊ ┊ ┊ ┊ ┊	112	┊ ┊ ┊ ┊ ┊
13	┊ ┊ ┊ ┊ ┊	38	┊ ┊ ┊ ┊ ┊	63	┊ ┊ ┊ ┊ ┊	88	┊ ┊ ┊ ┊ ┊	113	┊ ┊ ┊ ┊ ┊
14	┊ ┊ ┊ ┊ ┊	39	┊ ┊ ┊ ┊ ┊	64	┊ ┊ ┊ ┊ ┊	89	┊ ┊ ┊ ┊ ┊	114	┊ ┊ ┊ ┊ ┊
15	┊ ┊ ┊ ┊ ┊	40	┊ ┊ ┊ ┊ ┊	65	┊ ┊ ┊ ┊ ┊	90	┊ ┊ ┊ ┊ ┊	115	┊ ┊ ┊ ┊ ┊
16	┊ ┊ ┊ ┊ ┊	41	┊ ┊ ┊ ┊ ┊	66	┊ ┊ ┊ ┊ ┊	91	┊ ┊ ┊ ┊ ┊	116	┊ ┊ ┊ ┊ ┊
17	┊ ┊ ┊ ┊ ┊	42	┊ ┊ ┊ ┊ ┊	67	┊ ┊ ┊ ┊ ┊	92	┊ ┊ ┊ ┊ ┊	117	┊ ┊ ┊ ┊ ┊
18	┊ ┊ ┊ ┊ ┊	43	┊ ┊ ┊ ┊ ┊	68	┊ ┊ ┊ ┊ ┊	93	┊ ┊ ┊ ┊ ┊	118	┊ ┊ ┊ ┊ ┊
19	┊ ┊ ┊ ┊ ┊	44	┊ ┊ ┊ ┊ ┊	69	┊ ┊ ┊ ┊ ┊	94	┊ ┊ ┊ ┊ ┊	119	┊ ┊ ┊ ┊ ┊
20	┊ ┊ ┊ ┊ ┊	45	┊ ┊ ┊ ┊ ┊	70	┊ ┊ ┊ ┊ ┊	95	┊ ┊ ┊ ┊ ┊	120	┊ ┊ ┊ ┊ ┊
21	┊ ┊ ┊ ┊ ┊	46	┊ ┊ ┊ ┊ ┊	71	┊ ┊ ┊ ┊ ┊	96	┊ ┊ ┊ ┊ ┊	121	┊ ┊ ┊ ┊ ┊
22	┊ ┊ ┊ ┊ ┊	47	┊ ┊ ┊ ┊ ┊	72	┊ ┊ ┊ ┊ ┊	97	┊ ┊ ┊ ┊ ┊	122	┊ ┊ ┊ ┊ ┊
23	┊ ┊ ┊ ┊ ┊	48	┊ ┊ ┊ ┊ ┊	73	┊ ┊ ┊ ┊ ┊	98	┊ ┊ ┊ ┊ ┊	123	┊ ┊ ┊ ┊ ┊
24	┊ ┊ ┊ ┊ ┊	49	┊ ┊ ┊ ┊ ┊	74	┊ ┊ ┊ ┊ ┊	99	┊ ┊ ┊ ┊ ┊	124	┊ ┊ ┊ ┊ ┊
25	┊ ┊ ┊ ┊ ┊	50	┊ ┊ ┊ ┊ ┊	75	┊ ┊ ┊ ┊ ┊	100	┊ ┊ ┊ ┊ ┊	125	┊ ┊ ┊ ┊ ┊